Language, Schooling, and Society

Language, Schooling, and Society

Edited by
Stephen N. Tchudi

Proceedings, of the
International Federation for the
Teaching of English Seminar at
Michigan State University
November, 11-14, 1984

BOYNTON/COOK PUBLISHERS, INC.
UPPER MONTCLAIR, NEW JERSEY 07043

Library of Congress Cataloging-in-Publication Data

Main entry under title:

Language, schooling, and society.

  Proceedings of the Seminar of the International Federation for
the Teaching of English, held Nov. 11-14, 1984 at Michigan State
University.
  1. English language—Study and teaching—Congresses.
2. Language and languages—Study and teaching—Congresses.
3. Sociolinguistics—Congresses. 4. Language and education—
Congresses. I. Tchudi, Stephen, 1942-   . II. International
Federation for the Teaching of English.
PE1065.L36   1985   428'.007   85-21327
ISBN 0-86709-147-9

For information address Boynton/Cook Publishers, Inc.
52 Upper Montclair Plaza, P.O. Box 860, Upper Montclair, NJ 07043

Printed in the United States of America
85 86 87 88 10 9 8 7 6 5 4 3 2 1

Acknowledgments

The Seminar whose proceedings are reported in this volume was held on the campus of Michigan State University, East Lansing, Michigan, U.S.A. It was made possible, in part, through the generous grants and support of:

Michigan State University
    Office of the Provost
    College of Arts and Letters
    College of Education
    Department of English
    Canadian-American Studies Program
    Continuing Education Program
The Longview Foundation for World Understanding
The National Council of Teachers of English
The Canadian Consulate of Detroit
Oxford University Press
Boynton/Cook Publishers

Contents

Language, Schooling, and Society

Editor's Introduction

STEPHEN N. TCHUDI

Michigan State University (U.S.A.)

The International Federation for the Teaching of English (IFTE) was founded in Montreal, Canada in May of 1983, but it has a much longer history. Shortly after the Anglo-American Seminar on the Teaching of English, held at Dartmouth College in 1966, a group calling itself the International Steering Committee (ISC) was formed to continue the work begun at Dartmouth. The ISC subsequently held conferences in York, England (1970) and Sydney, Australia (1980) and expanded its membership beyond the National Council of Teachers of English (U.S.A.) and the National Association for the Teaching of English (U.K.) to include the English teaching organizations of Australia, New Zealand, and Canada.

At the 1983 Montreal meeting, the ISC executive board made several decisions affecting the future of the organization. It changed the name of the group to the more descriptive "International Federation for the Teaching of English," and it created a plan for more frequent meetings and conferences. Among the suggestions offered was that of IFTE "pre-conferences," held immediately preceding the national meetings of member organizations, on the assumption that many people interested might more easily obtain funding for two meetings than one. A "test" seminar held in Montreal in conjunction with the conference of the Canadian Council of Teachers of English was highly successful. The first seminar to be held under the IFTE name was conducted November 11–14, 1984 at Michigan State University, East Lansing, and the proceedings of that Seminar are the subject of this volume.

It was my pleasure as President of the National Council of Teachers of English to welcome IFTE delegates to my home campus and to serve with my colleague, Sheila Fitzgerald, then NCTE President-Elect, as convenor of the Seminar.

The conference theme grew from a recommendation of Anthony Adams of Cambridge University (U.K.), one of the founders of the International Steering Committee. Tony suggested that it was time for ISC/IFTE member organizations to take a critical look at the implications of the new electronic media for education, with special concern for the impact of microcomputers. In planning the Seminar, Sheila Fitzgerald and I felt it was time not only to look at electronic influences on language and learning, but to examine the broad functions of language and education in McLuhan's global village. Thus we developed the Seminar theme, "Language, Schooling, and Society."

A steering committee representing the IFTE member nations was created to draw up a list of invitees, of whom 128 eventually participated: 15 from Australia, 6 from New Zealand, 18 from Canada, 7 from Great Britain, one each from Scotland and Wales, and 80 from the host country, the United States. (The Seminar participants are listed in Appendix A.)

Prior to the Seminar, participants chose to join one of five study groups on the conference topics:

- Language and Public Affairs
- Language and Schooling
- Language and the New Media
- Language, Literature, and Human Values
- Language and Multicultural Education

Many members of the study groups prepared working papers for distribution and reading prior to the conference. Space did not permit publishing these papers as part of the conference proceedings. However, they are listed in Appendix B. Many of the papers have subsequently been accepted for publication in the journals of IFTE member organizations.

The Seminar itself consisted of a series of plenary or keynote addresses on the conference subtopics alternating with study group gatherings and nightly "cracker barrel" discussions. The keynote addresses are reprinted in Part I of this collection, "International Perspectives on Language, Schooling, and Society." The recommendations of the study groups appear in Part II, "Global Imperatives for Literacy and Learning in English."

The Seminar speakers and group leaders asked me to write an introduction looking at what they labeled the "horizontal" themes of the Seminar: those issues and concerns which cut across several or all of the study groups and speeches.

As I studied the various addresses and group reports, I first identified *seventeen* such horizontal themes. Although I like to create lists (a reviewer once accused me of having a "schoolmarmish addiction" to them), seventeen items seemed more than this introduction could bear. I therefore condensed my list and selected what seem to me the five most crucial issues emerging from the Seminar. I present these knowing full well that both the readers and the IFTE Seminar participants will see topics I have ignored or slighted. Nevertheless, I offer these five as a modest scaffold on which readers can build their appraisal of what happened in East Lansing and, more important, of what can and should be happening in the teaching of English worldwide.

1. *Exploring Beyond the New Orthodoxy.* Ian Pringle of Canada remarked in a closing address that "The ghost of Dartmouth is still with us." Although what happened at Dartmouth was, in a sense, predictable from the day John Locke gave the human mind a clean slate (or at least from the time John Dewey reflected on the relationships between experience and learning), Dartmouth has been a powerful influence on research and practice in the teaching of English.

At the same time, in an opening address to the IFTE Seminar, Anthony Adams suggested that it is now appropriate for the profession to move beyond Dartmouth, refining what we know and do in such areas as *oracy* (which, twenty years after Dartmouth, still remains pedagogical wishful thinking), *multicultural teaching, job skills* (a matter of political and economic necessity), *learning skills,* and Adams' particular interest, *microcomputers.* Many Seminar participants agreed that it is time to question the "new orthodoxy"— those widely accepted pedagogical tenets about a "personal growth" model that have become the currency of English education since Dartmouth—and to test its assumptions and limits.

Robert Pattison (U.S.A.) argued that the profession needs less dogmatism about its methods and a greater willingness to explore the dimensions of literacy and literacy instruction. Indeed, Pattison said we need to look critically at our definitions of and claims for literacy. In our zeal to make literacy a part of the whole curriculum, we may have confused it with all of learning, and in our eagerness to establish its connections with personal growth, we may have made claims for it that cannot be substantiated. He was especially suspicious of the claim that literacy *transforms* cultures, rather than being a reflection of or tool in cultural transformations.

A Dartmouth seminar probably comes but once a professional lifetime. The IFTE Seminarians saw no need to lay the ghost of Dartmouth to rest, but they clearly felt there is much to come and much to be done in English studies, that it is appropriate for our profession to embark on a new cycle of research, exploration, and experimental teaching as a way of refining the axioms of the new orthodoxy and creating some corollaries that will be appropriate for English teachers and learners as we approach century twenty-one.

2. *Teaching Values, Ethics, and Decision Making.* It is ironic that in some IFTE nations, "values schools" are those which aim at indoctrinating youngsters into a set of beliefs, generally conservative in politics, pedagogy, and religion. The Seminar participants came out foursquare in favor of the development of values and ethics in the schools, and they spoke out strongly as advocates of a central role for language and literature in teaching ethics. But the teaching they proposed was of a far different sort from that of the "values schools." In her keynote address, Louise Rosenblatt (U.S.A.) argued that "the aim in any educational or maturing process should be the development of the capacity to arrive at . . . a *considered* sense of values" (italics added). The Seminar participants agreed that what matters is not so much the values which students develop (though clearly the content of such values is important and can be explored through literature and language); rather, what is most important is that students learn the processes through which values can be developed.

This discussion of ethics in English studies was by no means limited to the traditional arena of literature. Tony Adams warned of the "immorality" of teachers' ignoring the use of microcomputers and their effects on students' thinking and valuing. The study group on "Language and the New Media," chaired by David England (U.S.A.), acknowledged that "English teachers will continue to value the literary traditions and conventional forms of expression," but added that teachers must recognize that "media change how we think, not just what we think."

Whether in discussions of literature or media, the term "empowerment" came up in many sessions. It seems to have originated with the study group on "Language, Literature, and Human Values," chaired by Garth Boomer (Australia), and it was defined as "enfranchisement," helping children be "learners and actors in the making of culture." The study group on "Language and Schooling," chaired by Elody Rathgen and Fred Johnson (New Zealand), even described English teachers as "emancipationists" because of their role in creating free and independent users of language.

All the study groups emphasized that empowerment could come about only through actual use of language, and John Dixon's castigation of "dummy run" teaching was often cited. Students should *use* the new media, not just study them; they should write literature as well as read it; they should *argue* for their beliefs and values, not just study language use and abuse. The Seminar seemed united on the point that the world sadly needs these enfranchised children. Whether the world *wants* them seemed a different matter altogether, and I will address it elsewhere.

3. *Teaching All Students.* Tony Adams characterized the 1960s as an age of "the pursuit of relevance," a time when the individual student was discovered (or rediscovered). The '70s, he said, evolved as the decade of "the pursuit of individual growth in the English classroom" as a clear outgrowth of Dartmouth. Among the IFTE participants, those '60s and '70s concepts were still alive. Dixon's study group on "Language and Public Affairs" celebrated the accomplishments of the "ordinary" student, and Seminar participants affirmed the notion that *all* students are fully capable of attaining a kind of literacy that will empower them to function well in school and society.

However, Adams also argued that the profession must now develop greater concern for the group and social nature of learning, tempering interest in the individual growth of individual students. The "Language and Schooling" group observed that "the [personal growth] model pays attention to both individual and social development, relating those carefully to one another."

In a keynote address, Frances Christie (Australia) argued that despite the expressed interest in "the student," our profession needs to extend post-Dartmouth research to understand more fully how children and institutions employ language, a theme echoed by John Dixon in his address. For many children, she said, language is still the "hidden curriculum" of schooling, and for the sake of those students, teachers must discover that curriculum and teach its "genres."

Christie also struck the theme of multicultural/multilingual learning that ran through the Seminar. "Language is often lost sight of among mother tongue specialists," she said, and it must not be ignored. The "Language and Public Affairs" group proposed an "International Bill of Rights" for student language learners (see the study group report in Part II), and the study group on "Language and Multicultural Education," chaired by Yetta Goodman (U.S.A.), asserted that "Multicultural education is not to be viewed as a form of remediation limited to ethnic minorities, nor as a superficial

awareness of minority cultures." As schoolhouses in IFTE member
nations become increasingly multicultural, the profession will need
to deepen its commitment to the students—*all* students.

4. *Teacher Education, Teacher Frustration, and Post-Dartmouth
Failures.* "Why are most schools going backwards?" James Moffett
(U.S.A.) asked in an address on "hidden impediments" to curriculum
reform. "Why are most schools retrenching into materials and methods long ago tried and found untrue?" Moffett was not alone in
questioning the failure of English educators to create wide-scale reform in the schools. Except in New Zealand, where a "personal
growth" curriculum has been a matter of state policy since the early
1970s, IFTE members reported that their efforts at reform have
been generally at odds with the interests and mandates of the people
in charge. John Dixon remarked on the "heartening" potential for
reform in English education, but regretted the "baleful economic
and political context that we live in." The "Language and Schooling" study group observed "a feeling of being right, but not yet
having carried the day," and its members worried about the "wash-
back" effect in the schools. Garth Boomer celebrated the accomplishments of a skillful "new way" teacher, but remarked that in
Australia she was not only cutting against the grain of public/politi-
cal views of proper education, but was "quite likely going against
the common practices of teachers in her own school."

It was easy enough for participants to identify teaching conditions as one cause of these problems. Overcrowded classrooms,
excessive teaching loads, and lack of materials all make it difficult
for competent teachers to implement a personal growth curriculum.
More important, however, were perceived failures of teacher training and retraining.

The New Zealanders reported that much of their success in
the '70s and '80s has been due to massive, "nationalized" training
in the early 1970s. The Americans reported the successes of the
National Writing Project in the 1980s as a way of bringing about a
modest revolution in composition instruction. Yet quality in-service
programs were seen as rare birds, and undergraduate teacher training
programs drew considerable criticism.

In a luncheon address, Mary Maguire (Canada) expressed her
concern that despite our knowledge of the non-linear and even intuitive nature of the learning process, a majority of teacher education and reeducation programs still rely on a formalist model. She
proposed a learn-by-doing-and-reflecting approach to teacher education, and her notion received support from the "Language and
Schooling" group, which called for opportunities for teachers to

gain "reflective control" of their teaching through analysis of experience.

Clearly, however, Seminar participants saw the greatest barriers to progress coming from outside the teaching profession. James Moffett raised the question of whether or not society truly wants the schools to create students who are literate in the fullest and best sense. More than one study group suggested that society seems to prefer students who clearly can function at a minimum skills level—who can, say, read and obey commands—but does not crave to have them raised to higher levels of skill, where their literacy might disrupt the political *status quo* through articulate criticism.

There was a fear, then, that the IFTE Seminar was yet another meeting of the "converted" preaching to one another and being self-congratulatory and/or self-flagellatory. The profession needs to learn to address "outsiders" more successfully. That imperative provides a direct transition to my fifth and last perceived horizontal theme of the Seminar.

5. *Acquiring Power.* "Empowerment" is a phrase that clearly has political overtones. It was not ordinary schoolhouse paranoia that led Seminar participants to perceive an *us* versus *them* antagonism in matters of English education and state. Most English educationists would argue that, in the long run, the general public need not fear students who are highly literate and capable of making independent decisions. Nevertheless, it was vividly clear that the central theme which lay beneath all Seminar discussions was *power* and *politics.*

In his closing remarks to the Seminar, Ian Pringle, incoming chair of IFTE and convenor of the international conference in Ottawa, 1986, said that he saw a need for "political action on a scale beyond any level at which I might hope to be effective." Group action is called for, he said, and he expressed his hope that this Seminar would be the start of more effective, unified action by the IFTE member nations.

To that end, the study group leaders agreed to focus their reports into the tightly worded recommendations and imperatives which are included in these proceedings. The leaders saw three audiences for these proposed actions:

First, the executive boards of the IFTE member organizations will be supplied with copies of this book. Our professional organizations are not, in general, politically sophisticated, yet if those executives act in concert, and if IFTE is effective in creating a worldwide network of English teachers (as proposed by the "Language and Schooling" group), there would seem potential for strong action.

Second, legislators and leaders in state education agencies and boards will receive copies of the proceedings, courtesy of IFTE. The keynote speeches of Part I provide the nonspecialist as well as the specialist a clear view of the international "state of the art" in English teaching; the recommendations of Part II offer an unmistakable program for action. The IFTE executives will make strong efforts to see that both parts are read and acted on by those in power.

Third, teachers in the member organizations of IFTE will have access to the proceedings through regular channels for distribution of publications.

It is this third audience, teachers around the world, that, in my view, holds the greatest potential for reform and growth in English teaching. Executive boards and legislative bodies move, at best, at a casual pace; even the benign bureaucracies of our English teaching organizations frequently need years to pass or mandate changes.

However, a great many of the imperatives urged by the study groups can be implemented immediately by individual teachers. There need be no delay, then, in beginning the sort of post-Dartmouth evolution called for in this book. As Mary Maguire suggested, the real key to change is teachers who will think carefully about their teaching and their students' learning.

It is my hope that readers will find this volume, first, provocative, enlightening, and even cautiously encouraging, and second, that they will use it as a document for discussion and individual and collective action. John Dixon and his study group members are right: "These are good times for the humanities, if we can make the work deserve the term."

Part I

International Perspectives on Language, Schooling, and Society

Keynote addresses presented at the Seminar of the International Federation for the Teaching of English and at the convention of the National Council of Teachers of English, November 11–18, 1984.

Language, Schooling, and Society:

1964-2004

ANTHONY ADAMS

Cambridge University (U.K.)

1964 was the year in which I first went to teach in a comprehensive school; it was also, incidentally, the year in which the National Association for the Teaching of English (NATE) first became established in the public eye. I went in that year as Head of the English Department of Churchfields School, a multi-purpose school with some two thousand pupils in the West Midlands. The new demands, now much more urgently with us, of urban education were just beginning to make themselves felt. It was the same period which saw the publication of the Walworth English syllabus of John Dixon, Simon Clements and Leslie Stratta in *Reflections*, a book which I, along with many others, seized upon with enthusiasm. It was also the era of David Holbrook's *English for Maturity*, a very different book, but one which was also alert to new problems facing us in the field of English teaching. The problems that we were all in our several ways seeking to identify then loom much larger now, twenty years on.

The first contrast to be made between the 1960s and the '80s seems to me the mood of optimism prevailing then. We really believed that the world could be transformed by education, including enlightened English teaching. Now, in 1984, the problems have gone a long way beyond anything that the schools can do. In England we have a structural unemployment that meant that fifty percent of last year's 16-year-old school leavers went straight into unemployment; in a one-time industrial city like Coventry, the figure is nearer eighty percent. Anything that we dare to say about education has first of all to be placed in this context. And, as always, economic recession is accompanied by a lack of public confidence in education in the naive assumption that it is somehow the fault of the schools that our young people cannot get jobs. So we have the parrot cries about the need to raise standards and massive media attacks upon

11

the failure of the schools to turn out the "products" needed by society. Jim Squire of the U.S. has reminded us that in 1982 the President of the United States set up a Task Force on education; and Jim seemed to see this as a hopeful sign of the public commitment to education, but I have to confess my doubts. After all, we had Project English in the wake of public anxiety after the launch of Sputnik, which led directly to the Dartmouth Seminar, but little, in the end, was really changed in the schools. However, I have in front of me the October 1984 issue of *CSSEDC Quarterly*, the publication of U.S. secondary English department heads, with reports from Colorado and Wyoming on "directions for excellence in English teaching" and these seem, in themselves, quite unexceptionable documents. Perhaps it is as well for us to take on board the necessity of making public statements of this kind for ourselves before others do it for us. In the past twenty years teachers of English have been far too reluctant to make their voices heard in the public arena. It will be a mark of the next twenty years that we shall need to "go public" in a much more determined manner.

More sinister, perhaps, have been some parallel developments in England, for example the recent report by Her Majesty's Inspectors on *English from 5–16*, published this autumn. Taken as it asks to be "as a whole," it makes some worthwhile points about English teaching, but this is not, of course, how it has been taken by press and public alike. It seems extraordinary that people with the experience of HMI should not have realized precisely the effect that the document was likely to have.

Chapter 2 occupies nine pages out of a thirty-two page document, and it deals with "objectives in English." There are thirty-three objectives for 7-year-olds; fifty-six for students aged 11; and fifty-eight for those aged 16. Amongst them, they include for 11-year-olds that they should:

> Exercise sufficient control over spelling, punctuation (at least the full stop, question mark and commas), syntax, and handwriting to communicate their meaning effectively.

They should also know:

> The functions and names of the main parts of speech (noun, pronoun, verb, adjective, and adverb), and be able to identify them in their own writing for the purpose of discussing what they have written.

This last paragraph seems to me to contain unbelievable linguistic ignorance. Apart from all we know by now about the futility of the teaching of formal grammar of an outmoded and discredited kind, one would have thought that if syntax is important, such items as conjunctions and prepositions might appear amongst "the main parts of speech." But like much else in the document the "discussion" of grammar bears little relevance to modern thinking in the area and ignores any real approach to language through an adequate model of language use. Rather, what is being recommended is a return to a kind of teaching and thinking about language that would have looked old-fashioned even in 1964.

The quotations above (taken as they are out of context) appeared in *The Guardian*, a newspaper which is reasonable so far as educational issues are concerned. Yet even it headlined the article: "Inspectors' Report urges uniformity of aims" and picked these items out for special comment. One can imagine what has been made of it by the more popular press and, indeed, by those English teachers who have seen in it an encouragement to return to the old curriculum and to dig all the dusty grammar books out of the stock cupboard.

Behind all this there seems to me to lie a number of very doubtful assumptions such as:

i. that it is possible to look at English, or any language, in an atomistic way:

ii. that it is possible, or desirable, in a highly complex society to have simple "uniformity of aims";

iii. that any good is done either by setting up National Task Forces or by producing papers like the HMI document. I rather agree with the leading article in *The Times Educational Supplement* on the matter, which was headed, "No Way to Raise Standards." Naturally all of us are in favor of raising standards in English teaching, and in education generally. I suspect we would all doubt that it can be done by such simplistic remedies or, indeed, that the disease is as bad or potentially terminal as our critics would suggest.

It was precisely the same kind of public unease that led in the early '60s to the Dartmouth Seminar, to which this gathering of the International Federation for the Teaching of English is, in many ways, a successor. I note with interest some continuity of membership between the two. I also note, with great pleasure, the widening constituency of the IFTE to include not just England and the United States, as was the case at Dartmouth, but also our colleagues in Canada, Australia and New Zealand, together with the ever-widening circle of those who use English as their official language, irrespective of what their first language may be. In the next twenty years one of our major tasks will be to weld together that international community of English speakers for which we have, at the very least, some responsibility.

Looking back, then, from the vantage point of today upon the period 1964–84 we may see it as a period of increased democratisation in education. In England, the growth of the comprehensive school was an important step in this direction; so, too was the development of mixed-ability teaching in which many of us in the IFTE nations then, and now, professed our faith. English teachers have played a central role in these developments and were amongst the first group to grasp what was happening. This led inevitably to an extension of the material introduced into the classroom in terms both of literature and of our attitudes to language.

In literature we saw a departure from what John Dixon has called "the cultural inheritance model," which led to a much greater use of modern and realistic literature, usually of the social realist kind. We found this in *Reflections* itself, and in the many other collections of the late '60s with abstract nouns as their titles, "Explorations," "Departures," "Encounters," and many more. Indeed, there was perhaps too much of a fashion for this kind of thing in the '60s and too little concern for the worthiness of the work of art in its own right. This has all become much more urgent and important in the '80s, however, especially given the multicultural nature of many of our societies. We shall need to widen still further the range of material that we bring into the classroom, to think in terms not of *English* literature but of *literature in English* as being at the centre of our concerns. Along with this we need also to return to a new concern with quality in the materials that we present to pupils in our classroom and to ask whether there is, in fact, any body of knowledge that we might expect them all to have in common. I confess to a slight feeling of anxiety when I find some of my own students, training to be English teachers, who have passed through a degree course in English without engaging with Chaucer or Shakespeare. Without returning entirely to the cultural inheritance model (which today has to be predicated with the question, "Whose culture?") we may want at least to enquire whether the absence of any common body of knowledge and experience of literature is a matter for some concern.

The welcome, and necessary, extension of the language curriculum reached its climax in the Bullock Report in the U.K. (London, HMSO, 1975), especially in that famous recommendation that "No child should be expected to cast off the language and culture of the home on crossing the threshold of the school." There has been an admirable extension of the range of language that is now considered appropriate in the classroom. This is clearly one area where there is much more general awareness and sense of responsibility amongst English teachers than in the '60s, although there is still too little real understanding of what to do about language work. (The HMI document, already discussed, mentions "language awareness" but in practice pays it only lip service.) We are going to need in the '80s in the initial and in-service preparation of English teachers to pay much more attention to giving them the knowledge and skills to handle the language curriculum, difficult though this will be to do without a thoroughgoing reform of much in the way of English courses in higher education.

Such developments, amongst others, have represented a pushing back of the frontiers of educational privilege so as to make access to educational progress available to an ever-widening range of students. However, on the other side is the constant flow of well-documented research from sociology showing the still restricted take-up of the opportunities for higher education by working class students, especially in the United Kingdom. At present, of course, given the economic and employment situation, there is an increasing mood of disillusionment with education at all amongst students drawn from all sections of society.

Throughout the same period, however, there has been a series of pressures designed to put this process of increased democratisation into reverse. The present dominatingly conservative mood in many of our societies represents a real threat to the advance of the past twenty years, and this is already being seen in many of the current officially expressed governmental initiatives in education, especially in the moves towards increased centralisation and governmental control.

The '60s might, then, in retrospect, be cited as a decade marked in English teaching by the pursuit of relevance, under the influence of Dixon and others; the '70s might be described as the decade of the pursuit of individual growth in English classrooms. Both approaches, with hindsight, we can now see as having been wanting.

"Growth" as a metaphor had an implied biological sense: provided the classroom could provide sufficient nurture, the process of individual growth would take place, the germination of the seed. In many respects this idea, already quite well established in English teaching circles (the first use of it of which I am aware is in Vicars Bell's book, *On Learning the English Tongue* [Faber and Faber, 1953]), was the last expression of the romantic approach to education typified by Rousseau and Wordsworth. It is to be found centrally in Marjorie Hourd's important book, *The Education of the Poetic Spirit* (Heinemann, 1949), and it is there even in the title of the early Holbrook's *English for Maturity* (Cambridge, 1961). For me, now, the main problem with the notion of "growth" as a metaphor is the emphasis it places upon individual progress and maturation. There is little sense here of the collective element in education, which I hope to show later to be centrally relevant to the concerns of the '80s and beyond.

Both "relevance" and "growth," in fact, can be seen as appropriate responses to the changes in society in the two decades they typified, but both were limited and are probably inadequate to meet the new challenges of the '80s, and the twenty years that lie ahead to bring us into the twenty-first century. It seems to me that we can now see certain things to have been seriously neglected in the period under review. These would include:

i. the lack of a proper theory and practice for language teaching, and, in particular, the continuing neglect of oracy in spite of the work of Wilkinson and others;

ii. the lack of any serious attention to communication studies, especially television studies;

iii. the lack of any adequate response to the changing needs of a multi-cultural society;

iv. the lack of a recognition of our need to educate students for under-employment, in particular the need to educate them in the ability to organise their own time;

v. the lack of any systematic teaching of study skills so that students can develop as autonomous learners, able to adapt and change as the society around them is adapting and changing. The one thing certain about the year 2000 is that it is impossible for us to imagine what it will be like, yet the students who will be coming to adulthood then are already in our schools.

I have commented on two of the most obvious challenges of the '80s: unemployment, and a pervading sense of crisis in education. Two other things remain to be considered. First amongst these are the possible effects of governmental policies of central control over education. This could all too easily lead us in the direction of increased centralism in other contexts and bring us closer to what we are particularly conscious of in 1984—the Orwellian nightmare. In this the role of language in the battle for men's minds is central. Two people, recently researching in Cambridge, have explored this issue. Marek has argued that the pressure towards revolution in his native Poland did not come from the intellectuals precisely because their education had excluded certain ideas from their consciousness, while Lerman has developed the concept of the "Institutional Voice" (IV). She has given the term "topic transformation" to its techniques of reality control. Describing her work in Aubrey and Chilton (1983), Chilton writes:

> The IV does not speak in its own personal capacity, but equates itself with its office or role, rather like the royal "we." It identifies its policies with "the good of all," "national security," "public interest," "our way of life" and so forth. It alone has the right to speak for the nation or institution; it is the repository of power and tradition; and it makes a unique claim to virtue. It thus has the ability to define events and people, and to assign a moral value to them. The IV accomplishes this by transforming the topics of discourse, by modifying or suppressing irksome political topics like unemployment, the nuclear arms race, the motive of the Falklands war. (In *Nineteen Eighty-Four in 1984*, Comedia Publishing Group, 1983)

In her work Lerman argues cogently that such ends are achieved by linguistic means which can be subjected to analysis, and that the political culture of the real 1984, underpinned by the press and the electronic media, privileges this voice to the virtual exclusion of alternative forms of reality from the public consciousness. We need now, in 1984, to ensure our survival, courses in language awareness that will seek to protect us as individuals, and as a society, from the insidious effects of the Institutional Voice and its effects on our thinking.

This links closely with my second consideration, the speed and significance of technological changes in our society. We need to find ways of taming Alan Turin's "universal machine," or (as we have come to know it) the computer in our society and the microcomputer in our schools. I have written at length elsewhere about the effect of the information revolution together with the need to develop our students as autonomous learners (see Adams and Jones, *Teaching Humanities in the Microelectronics Age*, Open University Press, 1983). I remain convinced that the way computer education is going in our society there is a real danger of our producing a computer educated elite, perhaps the Party of 1984, with the rest of us reduced to the status of proles. If we see computers in their right place as communications machines, we will realise that they are too important to be left in the hands of the mathematics and the science departments. It could be argued that not to involve ourselves as language arts teachers in the mid-1980s in a concern with computers is fundamentally immoral; that it is to leave our students as hostages in the world of the year 2000 and beyond.

The implications of the microtechnological revolution for English teaching includes, amongst much else, a realisation that the needs of reading and writing in our society will increase rather than diminish but that it will be screen reading and writing that will be the major means of communication in the future. We therefore need to equip our students will these skills alongside other literacy skills, something that we are failing in at the present time. We need to use the technologies of the present (already to be found in many of our students' homes) if schools are not to be seen as increasingly irrelevant to the next generation of young people. At present we are limited even in our teaching of keyboarding skills; just when we have begun, at last, to think about these, other methods of inputting data to the computer are making them irrelevant. We have to recognise that the day of the twenty dollar (or less) computer is just around the corner and that, within most of our teaching lifetimes, students will come to class with their own pocket computer and word processor just as they do with the calculator at present. This will also mean that they will have the potential of immediate access to databanks of information throughout the world; the importance of learning how to handle and process this, the ability to turn information into usable knowledge, will become fundamentally important. Already we are beginning to see how data-bases can bring up-to-date and primary source materials into our classrooms. Students will no longer need to rely upon the mediation of information via textbook and teacher but will be able to go to the source for themselves. As soon as this becomes universally possible it means that students will be able to form a new relationship with knowledge, and we shall have to rethink a good deal of what we have traditionally seen as the purpose of education.

We are also likely to see fundamental changes in the nature of literary texts, a changing relationship between writer and reader so that reading and writing become more reciprocal activities, the reader collaborating in a direct sense with the writer in the production of the final nature of the text—possibly, indeed, the idea of a "final version" may have to disappear altogether with all texts provisional and infinitely variable. Whatever forms develop in the future it is inconceivable that the nature of literature will not be changed by the biggest technological revolution in the field since the time of Gutenberg. (For further discussion of these issues see Chandler and Marcus, *Computers and Literacy*, Open University Press, 1985.)

Above all, the new machines, harnessed properly, can take away a good deal of the drudgery from our lives; we have available the possibility of a new Athenian Age with the machines replacing slaves and with ourselves having the opportunity to use our leisure more creatively and fully. This is why, at this time, education in and through the arts becomes ever more significant in our society. It is the arts that should be seen as the new "basics" of our time.

I would argue, therefore, that to meet the challenges of the 1980s and beyond the basic English curriculum has got to change greatly. These are some of the directions in which change must go:

i. towards a full engagement with the new technologies and their implications for communications strategies;

ii. towards a greater concern with group and collective experiences rather than a stress upon individualism—this may turn out to be one of the few continuing justifications for the existence of schooling in present-day society;

iii. towards more stress on oracy;

iv. towards more concern for writing and reading as a collaborative activity, something made possible only by the impact of the new technologies;

v. towards a greater stress on social and life skills and much less stress on the traditional "basics." This will include a much greater and more informed concern with both "communication studies" and "education for leisure," both of which come to be seen as much the same kind of thing.

To meet the needs of the new society purely cosmetic changes won't suffice. We shall need a new conception of education (not just schooling) which is one of a continuing, lifelong, community education.

In this, too, the new technology will have its part to play. One of the major social and political problems posed by the power of the computer is the question of access: How do we ensure that all have equal access to the power that such availability of information and power of communication represent? Already we are seeing in both England and Canada, and doubtless elsewhere, projects in community education which are seeking to place computers in the shopping centres and the supermarkets and to make them available to all at a nominal fee. It is important that this new source of information and power does become widely available and not remain the preserve of a privileged few.

The way forward lies in our evolving a full-blooded theory and practice of community education. This is not, of course, a new idea. One of its first pioneers was Henry Morris, Chief Education Officer for Cambridgeshire in the 1920s, in his "Memorandum on Village Colleges." (For further details of Morris' work see Harry Ree, *Educator Extraordinary: The Life and Achievement of Henry Morris*, Longmans, 1973; and *The Henry Morris Collection*, Cambridge University Press, 1984.) His words can still inspire us today:

> The Village College would change the whole face of education. As the community centre for the neighborhood it would provide for the whole man . . . It would not only be a training ground for the art of living but the place where life is lived, the environment of a genuine corporate life . . . There would be no leaving school, the child would enter at three and leave only in extreme old age . . . In it the conditions would be realised under which education would not be an escape from reality, but an enrichment and transformation of it. ("The Memorandum," 1924)

Morris' ideas have yet to find their fulfillment within our educational system, though some of our newer urban community schools are coming close to this. They represent the 1980s equivalent to that spirit of reform that inspired the work at Walworth and at Churchfields in the 1960s. The coming full implementation of Morris' ideas will mark, as Harry Ree has suggested, not just a new frontier in the extension of popular education but a move to a new shore, a whole new territory, in fact. It is only in this wider sense of community education that forms of schooling, as we have known them in the past, are likely to survive into the future.

Language and Schooling

FRANCES CHRISTIE

Deakin University (Australia)

Success in schools is largely a language matter—a matter that is, of capacity to interpret and manipulate the various patterns of discourse characteristic of the many kinds of knowledge, information and ideas schools value. Forms of knowledge, information, and ideas represent socially significant ways of working and of valuing, of addressing questions, and of answering them, of defining phenomena and of investigating and exploring these. Ways of knowing and of valuing, ways of defining and answering questions, are all, in fact, complex forms or patterns of behaviour, socially generated and sustained as part of the processes by which human beings construct and order the fabric of their collective lives, and hence make meanings. The various ways of knowing and of working, or of making meaning find expression in many different behavioural patterns, a number of them non-verbal, such as movement and dance, painting and music. Nonetheless the most pervasive and hence, I believe, the most important of the various behavioural patterns through which human beings make meanings is language. Certainly, in school situations, it is of central importance in the processes by which human beings seek to work and mean together.

It is the pervasive nature of language which is a principal source of many of the difficulties which creep into discussions both of language in general, and of language education in particular. Like many members of the wider community, teachers tend to take language for granted, focussing not upon the language used at any time, but upon what they describe as the "content" to be dealt with or the "information" to be taught. In fact, language is so much part of the patterns of interaction in which people engage that its significance is simply lost sight of, and its particular characteristic as a "system of signs" to use Saussure's term (1915, p. 16) remains unnoticed.

When people use language, they "sign" or make meaning, and they do so as Halliday has suggested (1976) in systematically ordered ways. They exercise options from the linguistic system available to them, though such options are not of course conscious, and they select linguistic items with which to structure and organise experience, information and ideas. The fact that language has the variety it has is indeed the measure that this is so. That is to say, the many texts—spoken and written—which it is possible to produce, represent differing ways of dealing with experience, either real or imaginary, or, if you prefer, either "concrete" or of the "inner world."

Language then, contrary to much popular belief, is not to be thought of primarily as a matter of words, nor is language learning to be thought of as a matter of learning words. Rather, language is a meaning system, where the operative consideration concerns the ways in which linguistic items are selected and patterned to create relevant meanings. Learning language, it follows, and again as Halliday (1975) originally suggested, involves learning *how* to manipulate the various linguistic items, creating patterns through which meanings are made.

Now ways of meaning are socially created, constituting the processes by which human beings constantly negotiate and construct their sense of themselves and of the social realities which they share. And successful entry to participation in one's society involves learning to recognise and to use its ways of meaning. While the processes of learning ways of meaning are no doubt lifelong, the point has particular implications for schooling and for the learning processes for which schools are responsible. Though the proposition is not normally put in these terms, I would argue that schools are actually responsible for teaching ways of meaning, ways of knowing, ways of working, and ways of enquiring—all of them socially created and socially relevant, and all of them finding expression in patterns of language.

Schools are conventionally thought of as institutions which exist to develop abilities of many kinds—abilities to think, to speculate, to explore, to inquire, to exercise discriminating judgments, and so on. There is a very general commitment in most English speaking countries—probably most Western countries—to the development of such abilities, and to the role of the school in promoting them. In practice, these abilities tend to be talked of in curriculum discussion and in much educational debate as abilities which operate in the head, and in some way independently of language. There is a well established tendency in our educational tradition to speak for example, of "cognitive development," or "affective development," or of "social" or "emotional" development, and of associated abilities in all these areas of development. Sometimes, language is spoken of as another area in which development takes place, so that in this view language is seen to have a status independent of, but perhaps of comparable significance to, that of the other areas of development. Elsewhere, but often in rather vague terms, language is seen to have some relationship to development in the other areas. Rarely, however, is it acknowledged that where people claim evidence for development in the areas identified, or for the presence of the associated mental abilities, such evidence is in fact largely a matter of language. Mental abilities of the kind I have referred to do not exist apart from the behavioural patterns, including in particular the patterns of language, in which they are realised.

There is a very good educational reason why the latter observation is of considerable importance in educational contexts. While we perpetuate a view that mental abilities operate in the head and separately from language, we see them as "innate," and by their nature not capable of much change. However, once we make the shift in thinking proposed here, we can view the abilities children are to develop in schools as part of a number of complex behavioural patterns they are to learn, and like anything else that is learned, these are subject to change. The shift in thinking involved is one which acknowledges the essentially social nature of human experience and of the processes by which human identity is shaped and defined.

Behind all the concerns with the development of mental abilities lies a commitment to individuals and to the development of individuals. This is a theme which has run through most of the significant publications on language and learning since the 1960s. If there has been an overall point of view about which the many authorities on language and learning since the '60s have probably agreed, it has been their general interest in language as a resource with which children express themselves and develop their individuality. The concern with individuality is important. However, discussion of the individual developing and expressing a personal point of view and attitude has frequently obscured discussion about *how* it is that persons achieve individuality.

Persons achieve identity and individuality, as Berger and Luckman (1966) among others in this century have demonstrated, by participation in social situations, by constant engagement in processes of building, affirming and reaffirming their collective sense of the reality they share. It is out of participation in these processes that persons define and give expression to the individuality which is theirs. In order so to participate, persons need to learn the ways of "signing"—the ways of shaping and of structuring experience and information—which are relevant.

I want to say something now about the nature of the structures humans create with language in the processes by which they build their shared understandings of reality, for it is relevant to getting closer to the ways of using language valued in schools. In the familiar and everyday patterns of daily living we interact with others, assuming roles vis-a-vis the various persons we encounter, negotiating, arguing, quarreling, agreeing, exchanging goods and services and information of many kinds. To do these things we constantly operate in various ways, the nature of which we have long since ceased to think about. For example, the patterns by which I daily interact with my neighbors, my colleagues, my family, and the numerous tradespeople and/or professional people whom I encounter in a typical week are on the whole patterns I take for granted, devoting to them little conscious consideration. Yet as is immediately clear if we reflect upon the matter for a moment, it is precisely because of the presence of such patterns of behaviour that interaction is made possible at all. The very fabric of life as we know it is centrally dependent upon the presence of these behavioural patterns. It is in these that we constantly define and give structure to our experience, and a principal resource in the processes of defining and structuring is the language system.

To the pattern or structure we create in language I shall give the name "genre," and like Martin (1984), I intend by this term to refer to any purposeful, staged, culturally created activity which finds expression in a language form. Such a use has some parallels with the more conventional uses of the word associated with literary studies, but it embraces a much wider range of forms than the term commonly refers to in literary discussions. It includes, for example, the countless patterns of casual conversation which people daily construct, as well as the reasonably formal process of text construction involved in producing this paper.

When we use language, then, we create systematically ordered passages of language, or texts, which have a generic shape or form. It is the capacity to interpret and create such forms or genres that is actually involved when we learn how to mean in language. Those who fail in schools are those who fail to master the genres of schooling: the ways of structuring and of dealing with experience which schools value in varying ways. Children who fail in schools are those who operate with ways of meaning different from those of schooling. One of a number of recent educational studies which provides general support for this proposition is that of Heath (1983). In a study of the life experiences and socialisation processes of children in three communities in the Appalachians, Heath has demonstrated the fundamental significance of language in the ways children are socialised, in the ways they develop a sense of identity including a sense of gender, and in the ways they approach and are prepared for schooling. Language plays a critically important role in determining who succeeds and who does not succeed in school.

In Australia, support for the same general proposition is amply provided by those who work with Australian Aboriginal children. Some Aboriginal children speak a mother tongue other than English, and for them English is a second language; others speak one of a number of Aboriginal non-standard English dialects. In either case, the children function with patterns of discourse and ways of working which simply do not accord with those of their white teachers. To assist Aboriginal children to learn the language of schooling—the language that is, of successful whites—is to assist them to gain a resource of essential importance in the processes by which they may become increasingly politically effective, particularly for example, in the drive for land rights.

When we look at children across the obvious differences created by colour and ethnicity, it is comparatively easy to acknowledge how critically important is language generally, and access to socially significant forms of language in particular, if the inequalities from which the children suffer are to be resolved. However—and this it is normally harder to encourage people to acknowledge—the same general principal applies for children of different socioeconomic groups within any one ethnic group. Thus, among mother tongue speakers of English, even where as often happens in Australia at least, dialect differences are not very pronounced, children from different social class backgrounds frequently operate with widely variable patterns of working and of meaning in their language.

So pervasive is language, and so intimately a part of the total patterns of interaction in which people engage in schools, that it simply slips from the forefront of teachers' attention. Language is much more readily lost sight of among mother tongue specialists than among second language specialists, for the very good reason that the latter are obliged to give some conscious attention to the language their students must learn. Most mother tongue teachers—whether specialists in the teaching of school subject English or specialists in the teaching of other school subjects—focus not upon language, but upon what they think of as the "issues," "ideas," or "content" to be dealt with, or the mental skills to be developed in their students. Yet issues, content or ideas are realised in language;

they do not have identity apart from language patterns, any more than the skills of concern have an identity apart from the behavioural patterns in which they find expression.

The issue is not that the children who fail *cannot* work in the ways that schools value and reward; the issue is rather that such children work in ways other than those valued by schooling. Their inability to follow and use the ways of meaning of schooling is frequently seen as a failure of some cognitive or mental kind, rather than an unacknowledged difference. It was this that Bernstein had in mind when he wrote that "children who have access to different speech-systems . . . may adopt quite different social and intellectual procedures despite a common potential." (1974, p. 125)

I want now to return to the notion of the "genre" as I referred to it earlier. For the remainder of this paper I intend:

i. to illustrate how in the school genres I shall examine particular patterns of language realise particular patterns of meaning;

ii. to argue that as a matter of their general professional preparedness teachers need a much more overt and explicit sense of the differences in patterns of meaning than is conventionally the case;

iii. to argue that school subjects or areas of enquiry and the learning of these, may be understood in fundamentally new ways, once the relationship between patterns of discourse and "content" is properly understood.

Spoken School Genres

I will begin by considering two spoken genres. There are several reasons for beginning with speech, though I will comment on one only. Most of us are familiar with the manner in which the term "genre" is used in literary discussion. Conventionally, the term refers to written language; I believe a preoccupation with written rather than spoken genres is a feature of our shared cultural traditions. A well established tendency to accord particular status and significance to the printed rather than the oral word has had the effect historically that we have become very insensitive to oral language. Unlike our forebears down perhaps to the end of the eighteenth century, and among whom rhetorical studies still had some value, and also unlike those traditional societies of the twentieth century to which writing has come late if at all, the major English-speaking societies have learned to attach authority and power to written language at the expense of serious interest in, or attention to, speech. The tendency is most apparent, for example, in the authority attaching to books and to book learning. It is also apparent in the way in which the grammar of written language is often invoked as authoritative in judging and sometimes condemning speech. How many of us, for example, have heard some passage of talk condemned as "ungrammatical" or "poorly expressed," when all that is involved is that the text *is* speech, not written language? The fact is that the grammatical rules invoked to make such judgments apply to written language on the whole, and not to speech at all.

We have been immensely enriched in one sense because of the spread of print materials which has been a particular feature of the nineteenth and twentieth centuries. In another sense, we have lost an awareness of the value and role of spoken language in our lives. (Not only are our judgments about speech often wrong, therefore, but I believe they are often wrong about written language as well, though that is a theme we cannot develop here.) In Australia, Hasan (in press) has demonstrated the presence of schematic structures in such casual speech as the service encounters in which people regularly engage. We can also demonstrate schematic structures in the patterns of speech found in schools. By uncovering a schematic structure we uncover a genre—one of the systematically patterned ways of making meaning in schools.

Consider then, Texts 1 and 2, both of which are extracts from the transcript of a much longer passage of spoken discourse, recorded in a grade 1 class of 6-year-old children. The curriculum activity was Morning News, or Show and Tell: a period of the day in which the children bring in items of their own to show and talk about them, or alternatively they simply have an item to share. This was a Monday morning, and some at least of the children were talking of things they had done at the weekend. Why can we identify these as representative of a particular kind of school genre? Because a clear ordered pattern of interaction is apparent, of a kind which applies with some variation whenever the teacher and children talk at this time of the day. The pattern is one which the teacher structures and indeed controls, though its presence is nonetheless only possible because of the co-operation of the children in bringing it into being: they share in the process of text construction.

Text 1

Mrs. B. All right, Karl, what have you got to tell us?
(Karl stands up from the cluster of children with whom he sits on the floor around Mrs. B. and moves to the front of the group.)
Karl: Good morning Mrs. B. Good morning girls and boys.

Chorus: Good morning Karl.
Karl: I saw Fairy Land when we were going to the bush, I did.
Mrs. B.: Do you mean Fairy Park?
Karl: Yes.
Mrs. B.: Did you go in?
Karl: No we just went past. 'nd we had a barbecue.
Mrs. B.: Oh what did you have to eat?
Karl: Sausages. . . . 'nd we saw some koalas.
Mrs. B.: Really . . . how many?
Karl: (hesitates, uncertain) Don't know.
Mrs. B.: Well that's nice. Did you have a good time?
(Karl nods his head)
Mrs. B.: Well that's good. Thank you Karl. Sit down.

Text 2
Mrs. B.: Danielle, you can pop out, please.
Danielle: Good morning Mrs. B. Good morning girls and boys.
Chorus: Good morning Danielle.
Danielle: I know something else to spell *(she whispers in Mrs. B.'s ear).*
Mrs. B.: Danielle said she knows how to spell another word. What is it?
Danielle: Mississippi.
Mrs. B.: How?
Danielle: (Said in a singsong voice) Mrs. M, Mrs. I, Mrs. SSI, Mrs. SSI, Mrs PPI.
Mrs. B.: Very good. Who taught you that?
Danielle: My Mum.
Mrs. B.: What was the word we learnt last week? Who remembers?
Danielle: Difficulty.
Mrs. B.: How do you spell that?
Danielle: (Said again in singsong voice) DI, FFI, CU, LTY.
Mrs. B.: That's very good. Any other news for us today?
(Danielle shakes her head)
Mrs. B.: Well thank you Danielle. You can sit down please.

A child is nominated by the teacher and he or she comes to the front of the group. The child begins by saying "good morning" to the teacher and the other children, though they have in fact all been at school for some forty minutes, and presumably did make whatever greetings young children do make among themselves. The greetings finished, the child in each case offers an observation about himself or herself—something he has done in Karl's case, something she can do in Danielle's. The teacher responds supportively, normally by asking a question of the child. Other children in the group may ask a question or make a comment—significantly normally addressed to the teacher, rather than to any other child. In Texts 1 and 2 no other child did make a comment. The child may go on to make additional observations and this the teacher will normally encourage. In practice however, the teacher normally asks further questions of the child, and she tends to make evaluative comments of various kinds— "that's good," "that's interesting," "aren't you clever?"—and so on.

It is a carefully structured pattern of discourse. Technically, there is present here a schematic structure, supporting the claim that there is present a school genre: teacher nominates child; child stands and moves to the front of the group; child makes greeting; children respond by greeting also; child offers observation(s); teacher offers evaluative comment(s) and/or asks a question or two; teacher thanks the child, who sits down.

The roles the participants assume are clearly apparent in the discourse patterns: they are part of the meanings being made. Thus, the child rarely if ever offers an evaluative comment. I can affirm this because of spending so much time in the classroom over many months, and recording the patterns of talk in Morning News as well as other portions of the day's curriculum activity. The teacher initiates and the child responds; the child makes observations, and the teacher makes evaluative comments. Of course, it is not the case that the child *cannot* make evaluative comments; it is rather the case that the terms of this curriculum genre cause the child not to offer such comments. Though she isn't conscious of it the teacher has generated the curriculum genre in such a way that it is her role to elicit observations and to make evaluative or supportive comment. The children's role is to make observations in response to the teacher's elicitations. In the cases of both Texts 1 and 2, then, the roles taken up and the expectations of persons attaching to these have consequences both for the choices of linguistic items and the patterns in which these are used.

All this is another way of saying that the ways of meaning which operate here require the production of certain kinds of texts, not others. In order to be successful participants in the production of such texts the children need to understand the nature of the choices to be exercised, and the ways of patterning and ordering language which are relevant. These latter observations, it should be noted, apply to all texts, and the very wide range of genres of which they are representative. They apply to spoken as well as written genres, and they apply as much for the wider community outside the school as for the school itself. In order to participate successfully in any context of situation at any time, one must understand the ways of making meaning which are relevant to it.

The ways of meaning valued and relevant for school learning are of course varied. Texts 1 and 2 are representative of one kind of spoken genre familiarly found, in Australia at least, in the educational experience of young children in their first years of schooling. Morning News or Show and Tell is intended to allow young children the opportunity to develop some fluency and confidence in using spoken language. Most of us will have some reservations about the usefulness of spoken genres of the kind I have examined.

My object in examining Texts 1 and 2 so quickly has been to demonstrate that there is in fact a generic structure—a way of making meaning—at work here. It is a way of making meaning which not all children concerned manipulate with equal skill, as my own research demonstrates. Some children slip with ease into the role of news-teller, both in this grade and in the parallel class of first grade children I also study in the same school. Such children relish the opportunity to speak, and are readily encouraged by the teacher to say more; some, indeed, need little or no encouragement, and will only finish when their teacher suggests that they have said enough, and that another child should have a turn. Other children—Karl is one such child—are eager to be selected and to tell, but they frequently have little to offer after a tentative beginning, and often flounder into silence. I have seen several children stop, unable to go on, and at least one little girl, who was eager to begin, became scarlet-faced in embarrassment after her opening and actually said "I don't know what else to say," after which she hastily retreated to her seat.

What I find impressive, whenever it happens that a child feels unable to proceed after a tentative opening, is that he or she never apparently lacks something to talk *about*. The difficulty, rather, is that the child does not know *how* to talk about it, at least in the terms required for the school genre involved. Hence the tendency to retreat into silence.

It may be objected that the genre is a poor one, not calculated to allow children to perform to great advantage, or alternatively, it may be objected that some children are naturally "quiet" or "not very vocal," and hence not likely to perform well. Let me take the second of these objections first. Some children no doubt *are* more or less talkative than others, but we should be very careful of the ways we use such observations when judging children in schools. Earlier reference was made to the experience of those working with Australian Aboriginal children. Such children have sometimes been known to spend some weeks in school without responding at all to their white teachers. Some white observers have sometimes therefore concluded that Aboriginal children "aren't very vocal." In fact, Aborigines as a people are as "vocal" as any other people, but as Harris (1980a; 1980b) has pointed out, they function with very different styles of interpersonal communication and ways of meaning from whites. The ways of meaning judged relevant and useful by their white teachers are frequently irrelevant, and sometimes incomprehensible to the children themselves.

Once this principle has been recognised for one group of children, its general force needs to be borne in mind for all groups of children. Some of the children in my study are of different ethnic groups and they certainly do often operate with different patterns of dealing with experience from those of their teachers. Others still, born of Australian families of Anglo-Saxon or Anglo-Celtic stock, also have different ways of working and expectations from their middle class teachers. It is too easy to assume that those who remain silent in schools are "not vocal." One has only to observe the children so labelled in situations in which they feel comfortable to realise how vocal they can really be.

Let me comment now on the other objection—namely, that the genre is itself a poor one. My own view about this is that the attempt to engage children in talking about their experience is not in itself valueless. The genre actually does assist some children. I have watched a number of children become adept at using it, and they have become in consequence quite confident in talking in a school situation. Because of prior and out of school experience, such children are equipped to respond fairly readily to their teacher's expectations and they thus enter with conviction and confidence into the pattern of talking about personal experience required. There are, however, more varied and challenging ways to involve these successful children in developing spoken language fluency in schools. Most of us could comment readily enough on some likely ways.

The educational problem that concerns me for the moment is not primarily the issue of whether we consider this a good or a poor genre. The problem is to encourage teachers and the educational profession at large to recognise that *a genre is present at all*. As earlier argued, people tend to ignore language—spoken language in particular. Hence, in situations such as those in which Texts 1 and 2 were produced, the tendency on the part of teachers is not to focus upon the kinds of behavioural patterns which apply—the ways of meaning in which participants are to engage if they are to be successful in meeting the requirements of the educational task. The tendency is simply to note that some children cope and some do not. Similarly, when they are a little older, and involved in learning the various so-called "content areas" of the curriculum, it will be noted that some master the "content area," while others do not. Those who perform well will be described as "intelligent," or "highly motivated," or something of the sort; those who perform badly will be variously described as "backward" or "slow" learners, or something similar. Neither kind of judgment throws much useful light upon the question of *why* it is that some children succeed in schools while others do not.

The single most important problem faced by those of us concerned with language education is this: to bring to the forefront of teachers' attention an awareness that learning in schools is a matter of learning ways of meaning, and that these ways find expression in particular patterns of discourse. Once teachers have begun to recognise this, several related courses of action are open to them. Firstly, they can begin to study the ways of meaning of their children, recognising and respecting patterns of language behaviour which differ from their own; secondly, they can learn to consider the various forms of "content" they aim to teach, analysing the language patterns particular to these, and building an explicit sense of them into their own teaching behaviour; thirdly, they can devise teaching/learning tasks in such a way that children will be assisted to learn the behaviour patterns, including the patterns of language behaviour, necessary to deal with those tasks. Serious commitment to the development of such education tasks would mean abandonment of much conventional school practice. For example, much more than is normally the case, teachers and students would actively collaborate in the definition of school tasks, and hence in the structuring of the learning experience involved. The generic structures to be used in language would thus become much more overtly an aspect of the educational agenda, negotiated between teacher and students, and forming an essential element in the teaching/learning process.

Let us now turn to some written school genres. In learning to write, as in learning to talk, there are generic patterns particular to the different ways of meaning or forms of knowledge valued and learned in schools. Such patterns are not unique to schools. On the contrary, they are themselves part of a wider set of culturally significant and valued ways of meaning.

The numerous bodies of enquiry variously referred to both in schools and elsewhere as "disciplines," "subjects," "content areas," and the like, all represent culturally significant ways of knowing or of meaning. That is to say, a body of knowledge is a way of defining phenomena and of addressing these, or a way of asking questions about experience, and of finding answers to them. Sometimes, the experiences dealt with are of the natural world, and the areas of enquiry involved belong to one or other of the so-called "natural sciences"; sometimes the experiences dealt with are of the social world, and the area of knowledge is one of the many social sciences. Sometimes the experiences are to do with imaginative exploration of personal experience, including that of the inner world, and the forms of knowledge in these cases are literary.

Whatever the broad area of enquiry within which people operate, and whatever the nature of the meanings they create, in order to make these meanings they actually manipulate certain generic patterns or forms. The point has important implications both for our view of the writing process, and our view of how children are taught to write.

Written School Genres

Some 6-year-old children in grade one—the parallel class to that in which the spoken genres were produced—were exploring the life cycle of chickens. Fertilised eggs had been introduced into the classroom and kept in an incubator until they hatched. In one lesson the teacher had introduced to the grade a book called *Egg to Chick* by M. E. Selsam. It was well illustrated and a reading of the text accompanying the illustrations provoked some lively discussion. One short passage from the book around which the discussion developed will indicate something of the nature of the experiences dealt with, and hence the kinds of meanings made. Talking of the fertilised egg, the book reads in part:

Text 3
The blood (in the egg) is full of food from the yolk. The tiny chick begins to grow. It is called an embryo. All animals are called embryos when they first being to grow.

The meanings of this little passage are scientific. The various experiential processes, which you will find are identified in the verbs used, offer observations about the states of *being* of chickens and embryos: "the blood *is* full"; "the chick *begins to grow*"; "it *is called* an embryo." Such experiential processes are one common characteristic of scientific/expository language: part in fact, of the ways scientific meanings are made. The text is written in the present tense—another common though not invariable feature of scientific writing, sometimes referred to as "the universal present tense." Overall, the

extract constitutes "factual" assertions about certain scientific phenomena. These are set out as generalisations of a verifiable kind, a
usual requirement of any observation deemed to be "scientific."

Texts 4 to 7 emerged from the writing activity which followed
the discussion of chickens and the reading of the book. The children
were given a series of little pictures depicting the life cycle of chickens, from egg to hatched chicken, and told to write "a little story"
about chickens. The series of pictures bore the caption "How a
Chicken Grows." In fact no child did write a story. Some attempted
it, and some didn't even try. That they were not actually successful
reflects no discredit upon the children. There is no intention to suggest particular discredit in the teacher, either, for she was functioning
with what is a fairly general lack of information either about the
linguistic patterning of stories, or indeed about any other genres.
However, with greater linguistic awareness herself the teacher would
certainly have been in a position the better to help her children master the written genre their learning activity here really required.

Text 4: Joel
Once upon a time a hen lay a egg inside the egg a chicken was
being born the chick eats the yolk it make(s) a little hole now
the chick is making a big crack.

In fact, encouraged by the preparatory talk about reading about
chickens, and, more specifically, encouraged by the nature of the
meanings they were actually involved in making, the children tended
toward scientific/expository genres. Joel, author of Text 4, did attempt to write a narrative, but the nature of the experience with
which he was dealing caused him to switch to scientific writing. In
consequence, what he wrote satisfies neither as narrative nor as exposition. Thus, he begins with a conventional narrative opening—
"once upon a time" and his selection of the indefinite article in re-
ferring to "a chicken" in clause one suggests that he is aware he is
creating an imaginative piece. He also begins in the past tense, a familiar feature of the stories or narratives Joel has frequently heard
read in school. However, at the third clause in the text, Joel moves
to the present tense, when he writes that "the chick eats the yolk."
Henceforth, the text remains in the present tense, and the meanings
are scientific.

Text 5: Simone
This is how a chicken grows first a Mother hen lays eggs then
the chicken inside gets bigger then the chicken starts to crack
a dotted line around the shell then the chick pushes out and

when the chicken is out it was all wet and when it has dryed it
gets yellow and fluffy   The end.

Simone, author of Text 5, makes clear from the start that she
is going to write exposition: "This is how a chicken grows," she
writes. Her choice of two indefinite articles to refer to "a chicken"
and "a mother hen" in the opening two clauses, as well as her choice
of the present tense, creates the sense that she is offering scientific
generalisation. Once only she uses the past tense towards the end of
her text, but she reverts to the present tense to conclude. As in normal scientific writing, a significant number of her experiential processes are to do with the state of being of the chicken: "it *gets* bigger";
"it *is* out"; "it *was* all wet."

Text 6: Susy
The mother hen is keeping the chicken warm under her feathers
on the egg and the chicken drinking the yolk and it is pecking
the shell and the chicken has pekt in a circle and naw is getting
droy and feathers and yellow to and naw he is troing to walk
but he Kant and naw he has got feathers.

Susy, author of Text 6, does something different again. Most
of the experiential processes in her text are in fact to do with action: "the chicken *is drinking* the yolk"; "it *is pecking* the shell";
"he *is trying to walk*," to mention some. Such processes are a
usual feature of narrative genres, for they are a necessary part of
the unfolding of events characteristic of narratives. Nonetheless,
this is not a narrative text, nor is it scientific exposition, as is
Simone's text. This is an example of a labelling genre, one in which
the author labels the series of pictures she has been given. This is
clear from the opening, in which she indicates she is not generalis-
ing about chickens; rather she talks of the particular chicken in
these pictures—"*the* mother hen is keeping the chicken warm,"
and a little later she writes that "*the* chicken (is) drinking the
yolk."

Text 7: Joseph
an . hen. lad . a . egg and. The., mudr sat . on . the . egg
and evri . dat . it got big. ar . and The cikn . peckt and .
at . lust . it cam at . it to twnione days

(A hen laid an egg and the mother sat on the egg and every
day it got bigger and the chicken pecked and at last it came
out. It took twenty-one days.)

Text 8: Stephen
The Greedy Giant and his dragon.
One early morning a giant woce (woke) up and went for a walk
without his breakfast he sed to his dragon would you like to
come with me for a walk then he remembered that he didn't
have his breakfast. he roared "Get me some bread or my dragon
will bern (burn) you" so the people ran and ran and got the
giant same (some) bread then he sed "get me same butter or
my dragon will bern you" so the people ran and ran and got
the giant same butter then he sed "get me same carrot or my
dragon will bern you" the giant didn't know that a bomb was
in the carrot and he exploded!

Of all the texts on chickens, Joseph's Text 7, is closest to narrative. It begins as a narrative, as is apparent from the choice of the
opening two indefinite articles—"an hen laid an egg." The experiential processes here are for the most part to do with action: "a hen
laid an egg"; "the mother *sat* on the egg"; "the chicken *pecked*";
"it came out." The text has a sense of temporal connectedness, and
it is written in the past tense. However, it lacks the sense of complication normally found in narrative texts.

An example of a text which I suggest does constitute narrative
is provided by Stephen in Text 8. This was inspired by a reading of
the children's story, *The Hungry Giant.* Text 8 has a number of experiential processes involving action: "a giant *woce* (woke) up"; "he
went for a walk"; "*get* me some bread"; "the people *ran* and *ran.*"
A series of events unfold that are temporally connected. These features, at least, Text 8 shares with Text 7. In terms of schematic
structure, however, Text 8 has a number of clearly marked stages
of a kind not found in Text 7. Thus, there is an opening orientation
in which the characters are introduced, and there is a subsequent
pattern in which—three times—a complication and a resolution are
introduced: the giant demands bread and gets it; he demands butter
and gets it; and finally, he demands a carrot, and gets it, but in an
unexpected way. Orientation, complication, and resolution—all according to Labov and Waletsky (1967) familiar features of spoken
narratives, and also, in my experience, regularly found in the narratives of young children's story books.

Overall, Text 8 qualifies as narrative. For Stephen who wrote
it, it was a story, he said. "I made up in my mind and then wrote
it." That comment is significant: he plainly saw himself as engaged
in imaginative or creative activity. Indeed, I believe he was too. Of
course, what he has written is derivative. Its derivative nature is in
fact an aspect we need to stress. Learning to write is one element of

learning *how* to mean, where that involves mastering various patterns
of language through which different kinds of meaning are realised.
Such patterns are culturally created; they are part of the sociocultural
contexts in which Stephen and his classmates must operate. Having
mastered a narrative generic pattern, Stephen is free to imagine any
kind of sequence of events or incidents he chooses within that pattern. With maturity and wider experience, he will no doubt master
other narrative genres, and in playing with the various narrative
genres available to him, he may well in time create new ones.

I have dwelt at some length on the texts concerning chickens
with a view to demonstrating that they are not representative of narrative genres, and I have sought to contrast them with Stephen's text
which I have argued does constitute narrative. I have done so because
I wanted to underline the point that the manner in which different
meanings are made is a matter of manipulating different discourse
patterns to create different kinds of genres. Scientific meanings to
do with experiences and phenomena of the natural world such as the
life cycle of chickens tend to involve patterns of the kind I have identified, say, in Simone's text. Imaginative exploration of experience
and, sometimes, creative reconstruction of the events of one's own
life tend to involve patterns of the kind I have identified in Stephen's
text. Both kinds of patterns are among the many that children need
to learn to be successful in school.

In the particular case I have cited, it was confusing to ask the
children to write "a little story" about chickens. The experiences
with which they were to deal, and the meanings they were involved
in making, were of a scientific kind; they were not the meanings of
narrative. Had the teacher had a more explicit sense of the kind of
generic structure required she could have focussed discussion upon
it, and enabled the children to master it the more effectively.

Language as the Hidden Curriculum of Schooling

It might be suggested that for children so young as the six-year-
olds I have been discussing the issue of whether they write a story
or not hardly matters: that what does matter is that the children
write at all, and that with experience they will get better. I find that
an unsatisfactory view. It seriously underestimates what young children can do, provided the generic structure they are to use is made
clear enough to them. In the study in which I am engaged and working with the two teachers involved, I have begun to demonstrate how
successfully 6-year-old children can master a range of genres once
they understand the features of the genres concerned. Such features

become part of the patterns of discussion about the writing activities; that is, the way of making meaning required for the learning task becomes an explicit item in the educational agenda.

Whether the point is acknowledged or not, successful writing at any time always involves mastery of a particular kind of genre. If its presence is not acknowledged by the teacher and hence explicitly built into the patterns of working in which teacher and students engage, it simply becomes part of the hidden curriculum of schooling.

It is the latter issue—language patterns as the hidden curriculum of schooling—which concerns me most of all. I have chosen to focus herein entirely upon texts produced by young children, partly because my own research has involved me of late working with such an age group, and partly because the relative simplicity of the texts produced by young children makes them manageable for a discussion of this sort. However, I would argue very strongly that the general conclusions to which I am pointing apply for all levels of schooling.

Somewhat earlier in this discussion I referred to the various "subjects," "content areas" or "bodies of enquiry" associated with schooling. These were identified as aspects of the ways of meaning and of knowing valued and of significance in our culture. Any body of enquiry involves defining phenomena and experiences of concern and addressing or exploring them. The point holds, incidentally, whether we are talking of traditional areas of enquiry such as history or physics, or of other areas of enquiry generated out of children's own interests. In either case a structured pattern of working will operate. The processes of defining, addressing and exploring phenomena involve ways of working, or complex patterns of behaviour, including patterns of behaviour in language. The behavioural processes to which I refer include of course "inner" or internalised patterns— what we commonly call thinking processes of many kinds. Mental activities arise because of participation in interaction with others, in processes of constantly negotiating and constructing various aspects of reality. The inner processes which develop are encoded in a variety of behavioural patterns, among which as I have already argued, language patterns must be considered of great importance.

There is a view sometimes expressed among specialists in language education that provided children are sufficiently immersed in really varied learning experiences they will simply develop the language patterns necessary for successful living and learning. It happens that such a policy does work for some of the children some of the time. The catch is that it works on the whole for those who are already advantaged anyway. The patterns of discourse of schooling and the ways of meaning implicit in these are generated by people who are themselves reasonably successful and advantaged—namely, teachers. Though they are not normally conscious of it, teachers work with expectations and patterns of behaviour which tend to accord more closely with those of some of their children than with others. Where teachers don't recognise how different are their own meaning patterns from those of numbers of their children, then they simply disadvantage the children concerned.

If we do in the future see a generation of teachers emerge with a lively and critical understanding of the role of language in the ways we mean, and hence in the ways children work and think in schools, we will witness considerable changes in the ways teachers and children work together.

As a first step, as I suggested earlier, teachers will become more responsive to, and tolerant of, ways of meaning among their children which differ from their own. Secondly in undertaking the analyses necessary to understand the kinds of language patterns children need to learn, they will be caused to reconsider much conventional teacher/student interaction. Out of the need to demystify the ways of meaning of schooling, they will be caused to abandon some, and to make others much more explicit and accessible. They will be caused to enter into different working relationships with their students. They will become much more actively collaborationist in the structuring of tasks and hence in the definition of the kinds of genres actually required for successful learning. Language will become no longer the hidden curriculum of schooling. Instead, its essential role in the structuring and organising of experience and information will be properly acknowledged. Whatever the age group taught, whatever the "content" of concern, whatever the mental skills to be developed, teachers will be able to consider and answer the question: What is it that my students need to be able to *do* in language in order to be successful in this learning activity?

REFERENCES

Berger, P. L. & Luckman, T. (1966). *The Social Construction of Reality*. Middlesex, U.K.: Penguin Books.

Bernstein, B. (1974). *Class Codes and Control, Vol. 1*(rev. ed). London: Routledge and Kegan Paul.

Halliday, M. A. K. (1975). *Learning How to Mean: Explorations in the Development of Language*. London: Edward Arnold.

Halliday, M. A. K. (ed, G. Kress) (1976). *System and Function in Language: Selected Papers*. London: Oxford University Press.

Harris, S., (1980a). *Culture and Learning: Tradition and Education in Northeast Arnhem Land.* Professional Services Branch, Northern Territory Department of Education, Australia.

Harris, S. (1980b). *Language and Learning Programs for Aborigines,* a video interview in the *Language Matters* Series 2 Video series. Canberra: Curriculum Development Centre.

Heath, S. B., (1983). *Ways with Words: Language, Life, and Work in Communities and Classrooms.* Cambridge, U.K.: Cambridge University Press.

Labov, W. & Waletsky, J., (1967). Narrative analysis: oral versions of personal experiences. In J. Helm (Ed.), *Essays on the Verbal and Visual Arts.* (Proceedings of the 1966 Annual Spring Meeting of the American Ethnological Society (pp. 12–14). Seattle: University of Washington Press.

Martin, J. R. (1984). Language, register and genre. In *Children Writing—Course Readings.* Victoria: Deakin University Press, Geelong.

Saussure, F. de (C. Bally & A. Sechehaye, Eds.) (1915). *Course in General Linguistics.* New York: McGraw-Hill.

Literacy: Confessions of a Heretic

ROBERT PATTISON

Long Island University (U.S.A.)

Some time ago, when I was reading a good many books about literacy, I discovered to my relief that most of these turned on a few orthodoxies unquestioningly accepted by the majority of authors. Once I knew this, I could leap whole libraries in a single bound. A few pages of most books would quickly inform me which pieties they subscribed to and which articles of faith they wished to elaborate. Out of a contrary nature, I found myself becoming a heretic in the temples of literacy—not just disagreeing with the conclusions in the books I read, but opposing the unspoken premises from which they were reached. I want to make a full confession of my heresy to you.

Heresy I

The first dogma I would like to dismantle is also the most fundamental article of faith in the credo of literacy. Dogma number one holds that literacy is a single skill like learning to type. This skill is a constant, and when the first-grader learns to read he is perfecting the same talent the priests of Ptah exercised along the banks of the Nile 3500 years ago. Because literacy is an immutable constant in the lives of cultures, we can measure it. Since we can measure it, we may discover that we have less of it than, say, the ancient Romans or the modern Swedes. Our comparative lack is then called "a literacy crisis." This much, I think, is dogma.

This dogma is an example of what Alfred North Whitehead called the fallacy of misplaced concreteness. We are so accustomed to talking about literacy as if it were a palpable part of the human condition that we have forgotten the word is only a name that we, not nature, have given to collections of events within our experience.

These events are connected because we want them to be, not because they are in any necessary way. The word "literacy" is our imaginative construct, not a definite physical reality like the amount of oxygen in this room. But when we see statistics measuring literacy, we make the understandable error of assuming there is something measurable at the other end of the measuring statistic. Often I think there is not, and the confusion about what literacy is has naturally produced a good deal of confusion about who has how much and what kind of it. I would like to begin, then, with the heretical notion that the term "literacy" should be stripped of all preconceived ideas and that we attempt to build a reliable definition of the word that both accords with experience and allows some leeway for the subjective dimension which is inescapably a part of the term.

The most vicious abuse to which the term is subjected is its identification with skill pure and simple. We now have "math literacy," "science literacy," "musical literacy," and "computer literacy." I recently attended a conference whose stated theme was "literacy." One speaker talked about color theory in modern art, and another compared television programming in Russia and the United States. Both claimed to be discussing literacy—the first was talking about art literacy and the second about media literacy. Needless to say, the conference ended as it began, in chaos and confusion—all of which could have been avoided had the participants been more careful with their key term. Once literacy becomes synonymous with any learned ability, the word is useless.

A narrower but equally misguided definition of literacy tells us that it is equivalent to the skills of reading and writing. But if literacy is merely a term to cover the ability to read and write, then we should follow Occam's principle and dispose of the word as redundant. Why multiply terms? Most of us, however, will not want to consign the word literacy to the nominalist scrapheap because we feel that there is in fact something useful and valid intended by the term, something different from mere reading and writing. Specifically, literacy must have to do with our ability to use language in our negotiations with the world. Reading and writing are two linguistic ways of conducting these negotiations, but they aren't the only ways. Literacy deals with the whole negotiation, not just a part of it.

Literacy describes a relation between ourselves as language users and the world we inhabit. We know that the world changes, and we know that our methods of negotiating with it also change, and that the change in one may be either cause or effect of change in the other. We live in what Whitehead called an organic world, a world of process, and it would be remarkable if literacy proved to be the one thing in this world that did *not* change.

Over two hundred years ago Lord Chesterfield defined literacy as knowledge of Greek and Latin. "Classical knowledge . . . is absolutely necessary for everybody," he said, and by "everybody" he presumably meant everybody who was anybody, because Chesterfield knew that he used his words the same way that he made his definitions—relatively. Chesterfield's definition of literacy seems to us useless, elitist, and narrow-minded; yet it is, I think, accurate precisely because it was relative. What led him to equate classical learning and literacy? "Because everybody has agreed to think and call it so," he said. Chesterfield was smart enough to see that literacy is whatever people make of their linguistic relations with the world, and his definition accurately describes the relationship called literacy as it existed among the English educated classes in 1748. We would do well to imitate Chesterfield's method when we ask what literacy is in our day and age and to proceed without reference to non-existent absolutes, imaginary crises, or fantastic methods of quantification.

Heresy II

In the second dogma I want to discuss, there are proper ways to teach people to be literate, and when we discover them, we can write proper textbooks taught in proper curricula, mastery of which will be measured by proper objective tests. In fact, we are already in sight of this happy day, and so much is now known about literacy and basic skills that new academic disciplines in these specializations have grown up around us. The kingdom is at hand.

I used to subscribe to this dogma myself when I first taught composition as an adjunct in a large factory of a junior college in the City University of New York system. I knew there was a proper way to teach students to be literate—and I knew that I knew it not. My senior colleagues all seemed to know the one true way, though each one true way was different from all the others. In the too-frequent faculty meetings held to discuss composition, I learned of many perfect methods: *The Lash*—drill and repetition punctuated by myriad D's and F's. *The Book*—one of my colleagues studiously wrote out the grammatical rule for each of her students' mechanical infractions and made them memorize it. *The Diary*—writing is only accomplished when the teacher reaches the students' innermost selves, and so the teacher must encourage the student to divulge as much of his or her personal life as possible. *The Wagon-Train Method*—practiced by the resident hippy: "Hey, everybody, put your desks in a circle and write something." Each teacher swore that his method produced spectacular results, while my efforts made so little headway that I finally turned to the head of the department for help. My class wasn't making any progress, I told her. She said hers wasn't either and recommended I wheel out the stereo and play them Beethoven—the *Beethoven Method.*

Some years and a trillion exam books later, I now know that as soon as anyone announces that he has tapped into ultimate truth about how to teach people to be literate, it's time to head for the door. In the intervening years I've had a chance to read essays produced by similar students working for similar lengths of time under each of these methods, and the essays they produce as a result are—remarkably similar. Let me try to account for this similarity and my hostility to method.

The dogma of proper method proceeds from the first dogma I discussed—that literacy is an immutable and measurable some*thing.* But it's not. Even in the brain, literacy is a complex of relationships between various areas of the nervous system used for talking, seeing, moving, remembering, suppressing, analyzing. You can remove large segments of these areas and still have a thinking, verbal human being. And so it is with literacy as well. You can attack literacy across its political frontier, and when you're done the patient may still be a functional human being, his literacy perhaps more political, emotional, or automatic than that of someone else, but not remarkably so, because the relationships of literacy are so much more complex than any one of their parts that the variations will hardly be noticeable if you concentrate only on a part.

You may object at this point that I have proved rather than refuted the dogma under discussion, because if literacy is a set of physical relationships in the brain and in life, these can be mapped and described, and we could have a department of literacy to tell us how to work the machinery in the most beneficial way.

Wrong. Despite Messrs. Chomsky and Fodor the brain does not work like a state-of-the-art computer. Unlike a machine, the brain cannot be isolated from experience. You can put a new computer in storage for five years, take it out, dust it off, and it will perform as well as new. If you try the same thing with a new-born baby—an experiment actually performed by a pharaoh of the twenty-sixth dynasty and by the Emperor Frederick II—you will wind up with a catatonic or a corpse. The so-called programming of the brain or of human language activity cannot take place without individual experiences, which are unique, and so every person's literacy, much less every nation's and every age's, is different and can only exist by being different. Literacy describes not only the abstract relations between human language and the world, but also must describe the jumble of individual and very material events that make up these abstracts in practice.

Because literacy describes not an ideal relationship but natural events in the history of nations and individuals, it is not possible to fix one method or even several correct methods by which it can be taught. But the dogma I am discussing holds that learning true methods is the goal—and lest you think I am inventing a dogma only to refute it, let me point to the trend in American higher education with regard to teaching basic literacy.

Faced with the so-called literacy crisis, American universities have responded by developing sub-departments in Composition, Rhetoric, Writing—they go by various names, but they share a common purpose. This new discipline is usually under the nominal control of the English department. You might well ask, Why doesn't the English department teach reading and writing like it used to do? There are several possible answers. I leave aside the cynical conjecture that tenured English faculty wish to create a teaching proletariat of composition instructors to relieve themselves of the unpleasant necessity of grading freshmen papers. Such things do not happen in the academic world, and we must ascribe the development of these new disciplines to purer motives, however misguided. I think the answer is that we now have English *and* composition departments as a result of the dogma I am attempting to dismantle: the belief that literacy is a skill best left to the competence of experts who understand its functioning the way an electrician knows wiring.

Now we hear that literacy too is a universal skill reduceable to neat and enduring truths. Now we discover that to teach someone to read or write it is not necessary to have any substantial topic to write or read about—it is sufficient to have mastered Reading and Writing in the abstract. And so we have two kinds of English graduate students as well—those who study Chaucer and learn to handle texts, and those who study theories of composition and learn to grade papers. What these latter drones will lack in academic glamor they are to make up in employment opportunities.

I would let nature take its course. I do not believe the complex relations that make up literacy can be reduced to anything less than the total of weirdly different human minds talking and writing to one another. I am persuaded that the more diverse linguistic methods we use to probe the more diverse subjects, the more literate we will be in the end.

Heresy III

My third heresy holds that, fancy theories about literacy to one side, reading and writing have materially added to progress. Any individual who can't read and write is excluded from the benefits of our civilization and is a danger to himself and society. The illiterate can't vote right, can't think right, can't get work, can't fill out forms, can't obey common written instructions. Therefore at a minimum we ought to concentrate on the universal attainment of these reading and writing skills at the highest possible level of proficiency.

Only a practicing sadist would disagree with this dogma, and yet . . . . I wonder about the unspoken assumptions that lie behind it. Everyone knows by now that despite the census bureau's assurance that ninety-nine percent of the population is literate, in fact . America and other English-speaking countries have large numbers of citizens who cannot read and write, and that many more citizens exercise these skills very imperfectly. Everyone, I think, is in favor of eradicating these pockets of ignorance. But it does not follow, as I think the dogmatists assume, that these unskilled citizens prove our society is regressing or that we are on the whole becoming stupider, or that lack of these skills in a fraction of the population is a threat to order and prosperity.

This pessimistic view would only be correct if reading and writing were the only ways in which citizens could be literate. But literacy is organic and multi-faceted, involving all our linguistic relations with life. Lord Melbourne wrote to Queen Victoria, "I don't know, ma'am, why they make all this fuss about education; none of the Pagets can read or write, and they get on well enough"—and they did: the Pagets made fine soldiers, generals, and admirals; they even produced an illiterate diplomat or two. Presumably they had redeeming virtues, even above wealth and an old name, and perhaps they even had redeeming *linguistic* virtues, like a talent for seeing through sham, a gift for public speaking, or a charming way of paying a compliment. These too are literate activities, nor are they to be despised. Ask yourselves whether you would prefer to have dinner with a mean-spirited scholar-maniac literate in twelve languages or an ebullient dropout whose only verbal attainments were wit, humor, and honesty. Those who do not read and write may still be literate in good and productive ways. Even it it's true that reading and writing skills in the general population are falling below some past standard, may the population not have increased its linguistic abilities in some other direction?

The difficulty of the dogma I am discussing is that it assumes the world is static, that the kind of literacy necessary for the industrial West a hundred years ago is the kind necessary for us today, and that we are failing because we do not live up to model of historical excellence. But a good appreciation of where we stand with literacy has to begin with a good definition of the word itself. If literacy describes our linguistic relations with ourselves and the world, before we can say there is a literacy crisis, we have first of all to say what is the total of our current linguistic relations and then explain how these are different from what would be most desirable for people in our situation.

An inventory of our current linguistic relations would take years, but I will name a few items I think it would contain: in spite of so-called functional illiteracy, we are a culture surfeited by print—everything from *TV Guide* to computer manuals and deconstructionist criticism. In addition, we have recently acquired electronic media that talk to us continually, bombarding us with language. We have new technologies that depend a great deal on written instruction, but we write less, send fewer personal letters and make phone calls instead. We worry more about the exact presentation of instructions and data, but we worry less about what people are saying and more about how they are saying it. Economically and scientifically, we worry that language should be logical, rational, and precise. Personally and politically, we care less what logical content words have and more about their emotive significance.

Many people find the world that emerges from this inventory repugnant and regressive. They dream of a literate utopia in which ordinary citizens read Henry James on the subway, write each other epigrammatic epistles, and engage over dinner in well-informed debate about disarmament and Baryshnikov's interpretation of Twyla Tharp. But do these visions constitute the linguistic relations best suited to the world in which we actually live?

I think not. Our world demands from us the capacity rapidly to adapt, both physically and mentally. The ideal world of rational book discourse envisioned by well-meaning humanists seems to me particularly ill-suited to the kinds of adaptation whole populations in the West have now to make. Linguistic relationships that are both more scientific and more emotional, more precise and more oral, more narrow and more diverse seem better suited to our situation. We need an exact and highly regimented literacy to survive the postindustrial economy. We also need a fluid, evanescent, and varied literacy to preserve our egalitarian revolution, which is one of the conditions of our economic success. I am suggesting that our society has evolved a complex literacy, no matter how odious to many of us, well-adapted to its needs.

I am not suggesting that we let reading and writing quietly slip out of the curriculum. They are essential in our current literacy for the transfer of certain kinds of information and to a lesser extent than in days of yore for debate and discussion. They are also essential for a minority of the population as a means of knowing the past, but this is a need not felt by the great majority of citizens. Every citizen should have the skills of reading and writing on the good Darwinian principle that the more varieties of anything including literacy you can generate, the surer the chance of survival will be. I am not attacking reading and writing. I am suggesting, though, that we should not confuse these two skills with literacy, which is bigger than either, or worry unnecessarily if the relation of reading and writing with the rest of life undergoes inevitable change or even diminution. Which brings me to my next and fourth dogma.

Heresy IV

In this dogma, we are told that television and other new media represent a threat to literacy and should be suppressed, controlled, or made to conform to the improvement of reading and writing. We are all familiar with the government committees that have investigated our literacy crisis and pointed the finger of blame at television, or the apostles of decency who denounce rock music's electronic domination of the airwaves as a return to the Paleolithic period.

In my heresy, I would like to suggest that the hysterical opponents of the new media are overreacting, even though their description of what's happening may be correct. Today's high school graduate writes and reads less than his counterpart of fifty years ago. I will go an extra step and admit that part of the reason he reads and writes less is that he spends a lot of time plugged in to earphones and watching television. Now from these admissions the orthodox party wants to conclude that today's graduate is less literate than his predecessor. And to that I say Nonsense. The dogmatist would be right if literacy were only reading and writing, but it isn't. To convince me that today's graduate is less literate, you would have to show me that his capacity to use language in dealing with the world was less than his forbears'. You would have to show me that what he had lost in reading and writing was not compensated by a gain somewhere else in his linguistic makeup. And you would have to show me that his use of language was less well-adapted to survival in his world than the literacy of his predecessor was to survival in the world of fifty years ago. I don't think the orthodox party can show me any of these things, and therefore I reject its dogma.

I have tried in these remarks to steer clear of statistics and surveys because they are so often flawed by imperfect definitions or simple prejudice. However, I have at hand a study that supports and I think elucidates my position, and of course it is flawless in method and presentation. My report comes from the California Department of Education. It is a study of 10,000 sixth-graders, their media habits, their social status, and their academic achievement. As the orthodox party anticipates, students from all backgrounds who spend inordinate amounts of time glued to the TV—that is more than four hours a day—perform very poorly in school. But the best performers are those who spend a moderate amount of time watching TV—between one and two hours a day.

When the students are separated according to the social status of their parents, however, we learn something even more interesting. Children whose parents' jobs are professional or managerial do worse in school the more they watch TV, but working-class children do better in school the more they watch, up to a limit of four hours a day. Or to interpret this result in terms of what I have been saying—children who have grown up with a traditional nineteenth-century kind of literacy are threatened by electronic media, while children who have no particular literacy to start with readily adapt to TV and improve their achievement under its influence.

Now I am delighted with this survey, not only because it confirms the classical adage about moderation in all things, but because it produces exactly the result my heresy anticipates. The world has changed and with it literacy has changed. Only a dullard would shun the possibilities inherent in radio, TV, records, and tapes, and only a dullard would embrace these to the exclusion of all other literate activities. The most literate students today are those who know how to read and write but also how to watch TV or listen to music and lyrics. And while the literacy of the children of the rich may be damaged by electronic media, the literacy of the poor can be improved by it. The new literacy is not only emotional and scientific all at once, it is also egalitarian and converging on a mean. I have no apology for the inherent mediocrity of the new literacy. I can only observe that it exists.

The dogmatist will object at this point that the bright student who watches and listens as well as reads and writes is still less literate than his earlier counterpart. He will say that TV is full of cheap sentimentalism, lurid violence, tawdry exploitation, and political lies. Reading, on the other hand, would make this student more rational, more self-reliant, more cultured. I can only deal here with a finite number of heresies, and so I am going to let pass the notion that reading and writing are rational activities that purify the mind (as if one hundred years ago newspapers did not publish much worse trash than appears now on TV, or as if in the Renaissance people read books and never felt an emotion below the hypothalamus). I will let that one pass, and will concede for the sake of argument that our modern students are not as rational, self-reliant, or cultured as their counterparts. But are rational, self-reliant, cultured individuals what the present age requires? Our age is at once highly pragmatic and highly irrational. Socially it requires interdependence of thought, emotion, and activity, not self-reliance. To make organic, complex Western society function at its best, it is probably wise to have an egalitarian literacy well founded in oral communication, in the use of language to project irrational human impulses, and in the dissemination of common and even vulgar thoughts, opinions, and feelings. Television is full of these, and students who didn't master TV as part of their literacy would be at a great disadvantage in our world. This heresy leads me naturally to the last dogma I would like to discuss.

Heresy V

Let's call this one the Huck Finn dogma. I name it that in honor of the high Washington functionary with whom I recently sat on a panel discussing literacy. Stated briefly, the dogma is that literacy requires the superimposition of a good humanistic education upon the fundamentals of reading and writing. The top functionary who gave such eloquent expression to this particular piety maintains that there is altogether too much of what he calls "Huck-Finnism" in America today—you will recall Huck Finn didn't know who Moses was, in or out of the bulrushes, and didn't take no stock in dead people anyway. The top functionary lamented the existence of such an attitude as an affront to eternal wisdom and a heavy blow at the future of the Republic. I asked him—and I am very fortunate to be able to tell you *exactly* what I asked him because not only was this discussion taped, but a public stenographer repeated it verbatim into a second recording device as it took place, thus proving that orality is alive and well in the heart of our book culture—I asked him, "Are you really saying that if you had Huck Finn in your classroom you would want to beat that out of him?"—my "that" meaning his dis-

respect for book learning and history in general—and our functionary answered, "You bet I would."

My heresy begins with the proposition that while many cultures
may profitably include history and book learning—what we call good
humanistic education—within their definition of literacy, to do so is
neither mandatory nor always wise. Huck Finn is in fact the perfect
example of why the functionary's dogma ought to be discarded.
Huck certainly has nothing like a good humanistic education. He
wants no part of school, he doesn't care much for reading, and he
certainly is no writer. The only distinction Huck can claim is to be
the narrator of one of the handful of books in serious contention
for the title of the great American novel. Poor illiterate Huck! Lacking all those good values, he is the most brilliant speaker in the
American tradition. He is the only character in the book who truly
possesses the humanistic values others are constantly proclaiming he
will never have until he is "sivilized."

Lurking behind this dogma and the others I have discussed is a
dreary supposition about human nature that Mark Twain rejected—
and I think he was right. This hidden supposition maintains that people, especially students, are the passive recipients of experience.
Leave a child in front of the TV, and he will get a TV mind. Teach
a child the wrong literacy, and he will know only that bad literacy.
Fail to instruct him in humanistic values, and he will have no values
at all. I find this view of life very disturbing. But my organic instincts
tell me that this latent premise of so much dogma about literacy is
false. We are active participants in the world. Children come to
school with expectations about literacy and with their notions of
language well formed. We know that if you try to change curricula
in ways that make no sense to students or their parents they will
find ways to prevent you. Huck Finn, even without a good humanistic education, had nonetheless attained a very remarkable literacy.
Is it not possible that the modern population, like Huck Finn, has
its own literacy, quite apart from what we may aspire to teach it?

American education pays lip-service to the greatness of Twain
while scrupulously ignoring his seemingly grotesque lapses into anti-
intellectualism. In my remarks, I am not even hinting that children
be hoisted onto rafts and launched down the river as an alternate
form of education—though in some cases the alternative could be
no worse than what they are now getting. But I would like to rescue
what I consider to be the heretical vigor of Twain's thought: that
left more to its own devices, our literacy will change and evolve,
and that there is indeed a native vigor about literacy that will survive
all our make-believe crises.

"Now," you may be saying, "he's really gone off the deep end of Philistinism." I hear a dogmatist saying to me, "One can't just sit and do nothing. True, we are not saving humanity and perhaps we make mistakes, but we do what we can, and—we are right. The loftiest and most sacred task of a cultured person is to serve his neighbors." The dogmatist who said this is Lida in Checkov's story "The House with the Mansard." Lida is a young lady of wealth and liberal sentiments whose mission in life is the gradual improvement of the human condition, and to her and her kind what I am saying is rankest heresy. I can do no better in defending myself than quote the sad hero of Checkov's story, who is the butt of Lida's invective: "Peasant literacy," he said,

> books full of wretched moralizings and popular maxims, and medical-aid posts can no more lessen their ignorance or their mortality rate than the light from your window can light up this huge garden. . . . You give them nothing, merely by your interfering in the lives of these people creating fresh demands, fresh motives for working. . . . Free them from coarse, physical toil and then you will see the mockery that these books . . . really are.

In the end I want more not less than the dogmatists. People will take care of their own literacy if given the freedom to take care of themselves. If we worried less about reading and writing and more about ridding the world of coarse oppressions of the spirit, then I think literacy would take care of itself, because people naturally seek to perfect their most human attribute, the ability to use language.

Teaching English 1984

JOHN DIXON

London, England (U.K.)

At the time George Orwell conceived his novel *1984* I was a very young university student—an ex-schoolboy among thousands of veterans returning almost daily from Burma, North Africa, Italy and central Europe. There were—I'm happy to remember—GI friends among us too, living in a temporary Army college outside Oxford and studying with us as they waited to return home. We were young, and we had emerged alive from six years of global war. Bliss was it in that dawn!

If I look back to what *we* (unlike Orwell) expected of 1984 and compare it with the reality, what do I see? On the one hand potential beyond our imagination. Thus, for instance, I can go into certain classrooms today in New Zealand, Australia, Canada, the States and the U.K. and see work being done there by "average" students that far outstrips the wildest hopes we had conceived in 1945 of students' educational achievement. On the other hand, stepping outside the schools, talking with people in their neighborhoods, and looking around at the global village I see equally the shattering of the post-war hopes millions of us had for economic and social justice across the world. In my own country, for example, over the past two years more than half our students have left school with no hope of getting a full-time job. The political and economic failure this represents has its social costs, but these are being paid today by the unemployed and the educational system, not by those who control the centres of power and the media of communication.

These remarks were delivered at the 74th annual convention of the National Council of Teachers of English in Detroit, Michigan, immediately following the IFTE seminar. John Dixon was a study group leader at the IFTE meeting (see his report elsewhere in this volume). He was also a chronicler of the Dartmouth seminar in *Growth Through English* (NCTE and NATE, 1968).

It is this gaping division between on the one hand English teaching and its heartening potential in 1984 and on the other the baleful economic and political context that we live in that inevitably frames my speech. But I come here to speak first of the achievements in education—international achievements, within the reach of all present here—and secondly I come to speak of the English teacher's right to support, the right for backing and resources to make these achievements accessible to the majority of students in the next five years. What kinds of achievement? What kinds of support? Let us start by tackling those questions.

English, I suggest, offers students the opportunity to learn in three ways: from direct experience; through drama or simulation; and from reading, listening or viewing. In the long term it is the lessons of firsthand experience that inexorably shape us as people, but as a writer I should be the last to diminish the lessons we learn from others—what people say, write or present to us visually via machines. It is lessons of the second kind that create our individual images of the global village we belong to, and which increasingly shape the social roles we are equipped to play in it. Drama—and imaginative play in general—offers a bridge between the known, firsthand experience, and the alien world beyond it: through drama we act out what it might be like to live differently.

So in studying what pioneering students are achieving, we must try to discover how they are learning from experience, how they are learning through drama, and how they are learning through reading . . . and how these three activities are potentially related.

Let us start in the elementary school, where it all begins anyway. I will take you into a school in Bradford—the British Detroit of 1884—a school set in the middle of a blue-collar area, where the parents have had strong and confident relations with the teachers over several years. As part of a writing project with a local unit, a nine-year-old class has gathered in a circle to listen to and exchange stories about animals. On this particular day Louise writes with more than usual care and this is the story she brings to share with her teacher, Michael Dwyer, and Irene Farmer, from the local Language Development Unit.

About my pet cat

One night I had just come in from playing out. I was in for a short time when somebody knocked on the door. I went to answer it and it was my babysitter and my babysitter's friend, and they said "Has your Starsky gone out?" I said "Yea." Then she said "There is a cat lying on the edge of the pavement and it is black and white and just the same as Starsky." So in the morning when I was going to school I knew it must be Starsky because he didn't come in that night. Then I went down and knelt beside him and it was him, I could tell, and I started to cry and then my Mum said "Don't get yourself upset. There's nothing we can do now." Then at school I couldn't do my work because I was so upset about it and then when I came home from school he wasn't there. So when I got in my Mum said "Why have you got tears in your eyes?" and I said "Because he has gone." She said, "I know. I rang the R.S.P.C.A. to come and take him away." And from that day I never forget him.

"Stories from Personal Experience 9–11" *Language Development Unit.*
1981, Bretton Hall College, Wakefield, U.K.

What do we stand to learn from this story, set alongside many others from the class? To begin with, I think, that experiences we all suffer or enjoy—that puzzle, disturb or intrigue us; that fill us with dismay or satisfaction and pleasure—are the basis for the "story of our lives," which we all keep on endlessly rehearsing or revising to anyone we can trust to listen with care.

In this particular story, there were important feelings to express and to contemplate. Indeed, if we had time to look closely, you would see that the structure of the story is a sequence of feelings: apprehension, dread, the outbreak of grief and the continuing pain of loss . . . Finding the words to articulate such feelings is not easy; indeed there's still something miraculous for me in the way Louise, an ordinary nine-year-old, manages to do so. She's taking language quite a long way, isn't she, into one of its fundamental tasks, the deeper understanding of our inner life and our relationships with others.

Louise's evidence of how students learn from experience is fascinating in its own right, then. But because of the work of the last fifteen years, I can now begin to place it on paths of development that move right through high school. I now realise how inner thoughts and feelings can be increasingly integrated by the story-teller into the web of events. I see how the other characters (like Louise's mother) begin to be rounded out and take on a life of their own. I recognise the subtler force of dramatic exchanges between them and the story-teller. And—whether in fictional or autobiographical stories—I sense that the story-teller is progressively more able to contemplate and review the events with a special kind of detachment. In other words, I can trace language being used with increasing delicacy and control for some central human purposes.

This is one branch of the achievements of pioneering students and teachers that ought to be celebrated today. Still remaining within the elementary school years, I want to add a second branch, one that forms when young students begin to observe and question experiences, and to seek help in those enquiries from books. The example that springs to mind will be familiar to many of you; it comes from Lynda Chittenden's account, set in her California school, of the making of a class book on whales. One of my most rewarding sessions this summer in working with a group of U.S. teachers was spent looking sentence by sentence at the following piece by a ten-year-old, Peggy.

> One awful thing to think about is—what is it like to be in captivity? You see the Orca jump and perform for thousands of people only because someone signaled him to do it. But, have you ever seen the Killer Whale when the people are gone and he's not performing? He's there swimming slowly around and around, not able to use his sonar and get the different and interesting sounds of home, but only able to get the same sharp and boring vibrations of his cement tank. But not only his sound world is gone—his beautiful dorsal fin is now flabby and dropped with no beauty anymore. In his tank he doesn't get enough exercise to keep it high and erect like an Orca in the wild.
>
> Next time you see a marine animal perform for lots of people ask yourself, "Would you give up the free and glistening waters of home for this?"

"What If All the Whales Are Gone . . ." Lynda Chittenden in *What's Going On? Language/Learning Episodes in British and American Classrooms.* M. Barr, P. D'Arcy & M. K. Healy, Eds. 1982, Boynton/Cook Publishers.

What did we find in this second branch of writing? First, we noticed how fluently Peggy moves from the abstract and generalised question—what is it like to be in captivity?—to the concreteness of "Have you ever seen . . . ?" She's presenting a real living creature, and even that word "you" draws us readers in, to contemplate it alongside her. But the picture she offers is powerfully structured by ideas, we discovered; there's one world which is sharp, boring and cement-like opposed to another which is free, wild, glistening—and *home.* This undercurrent of ideas makes a powerful appeal to the readers and guides their feelings. Her voice is there, and its strong emotional involvement flows through the subtle rhythms of the passage. The factual information she has derived from books (about Orcas, Killer Whales, sonar, dorsal fins and marine animals) has been all transformed into personal understanding for a real purpose—to have her say about a human issue.

This, we began to realise, was a *real* "expository paragraph." It is a challenge to the long tradition of sham exercises—dummy runs—which never offer a real audience to be convinced, persuaded, or informed by the ordinary student. It is also a superb lesson, along with other pieces from Peggy's class, about the true sources of informative and persuasive writing.

Such work raises issues about the potential development of informative and persuasive writing through the high school years. It points to some of the key questions we must ask:

- How is reading integrated with observation and enquiry?
- How is information for others transformed into personal understanding?
- How are the traditions of literary prose internalised by ordinary students until they are used with the same freedom as Louise's oral tradition?

So far as Britain is concerned, I don't believe we yet have sufficient published examples of ordinary high school students who have handled this branch of writing with the confidence and flair of Peggy and her class. I know personally that the breakthrough is being made—I've heard it from pioneering teachers in London, Yorkshire, Cumbria and even, most recently, Alaska!—but there's still a profound need to assemble more evidence, so that we can chart the developmental paths through from Peggy at 10 to students of 17–18.

Nevertheless, we *do* have a strong sense of what's on the horizon. If I had time I could lay out here a wide range of achievements from ordinary students of 17+ —achievements which would have seemed incredible to students of my own generation in 1945, but which colleagues across the world are now showing to be possible, given the right context. I must content myself with two.

The first comes from an inner-city school in London. In a project meeting the teacher, Sue Crump, had been discussing Studs Terkel's radio interviews in Chicago, brought together a few years back in his book called *Working*. With Junior and his class she had then looked carefully at three of those interviews and what people had to say. What the class learnt from that reading was to prepare enthusiastically to go out and interview people themselves—to learn by listening. Here is part of Junior's report of what he learnt.

Lois is a state registered nurse and now holds a nursing sister's post . . . Lois is twenty-seven-years old and is married. She is attractive and friendly. . . .

I wanted to know what she really did in working hours in detail. She does her rounds in the morning, reads out reports to nurses (male and female), gives nurses their duties for the day, watches students and pupils use equipment and machines, also makes sure that pupils and student nurses do the right things required. During the afternoons she sets tests (written and practical) for the students and pupils to do and gives them small lectures. After what she told me I said, "A lot of the students must be frightened of you." She said she makes them feel comfortable and she lets them feel free to ask questions. She tries not to be a bullish ward sister as she remembers that when she was doing her training she felt nervous at times and did stupid things. I asked her if she ever lost her temper during working hours. She replied "No." The only time she lost her temper was when she was a student nurse and a patient threw dirty toilet paper at her. . . .

Sometimes we wonder what makes people choose their jobs. In Lois's case her mother always brought up the subject, as she did nursing. She felt odd when she started her training as she never fancied nursing but eventually she got the hang of it and when she got involved it was too late to opt out. . . . When she gets her holidays (six weeks) she misses the place and always looks forward to getting back on the ward.

That may depress some people, she says, but she has done that sort of work for quite a while and it would take her ages before she could adjust to another job, as she has done this since leaving school. She says many men and women can't stand the sight of hospitals but its different when you actually work in one. People who make these remarks usually go to hospitals to visit someone or have a medical but when you work in one it's just the same friendly atmosphere as a school, office or factory.

Her advice to young men and women is that nursing is a good profession and you don't have to stick to one place or hospital. Nurses are always wanted at hospitals all over the world, and once you're qualified you can earn good money in many other countries. Lois also emphasized that there are many other courses in the nursing field you can do, she says you can always get to the top if you work hard and further your education, as she is hoping to do. . . .

I enjoyed talking to Lois and as you can see she enjoys her job although it was not her choice but she made a go of it and reached somewhere. To end the interview she said she was

scared of leaving school to start a life of her own but nursing
is her profession now and it would be a waste of time to change
it for something else. She can still remember that day, years ago
now, when she went onto the hospital ward for the first time,
after a six weeks introductory course in nursing school, when
she pinned on her cap and the patients called her "Nurse."

Education 16-19: the Role of English & Communication p. 123. John
Dixon (with John Brown & Dorothy Barnes), 1979, Macmillan Education.

A person with life experience is a book who can answer your
questions. That's how roughly half of our learning in life is done, I
suppose. So the thinking behind the questioning is vital. By real enquiry, Junior has learnt to do some crucial things here. He has integrated two points of view, the beginner's and the veteran's: both are
important to him, and to his readers in school. He has caught some
formative moments in the nurse's development—quite vividly. He
has encouraged personal reflectiveness, both from Lois and himself.
And he has turned an enjoyable personal enquiry into something
that is subtly and tactfully informative for real readers in his classroom and beyond. By the time this piece was redrafted I feel Junior
was viewing that encounter with an experienced adult on something
close to equal terms. His youthful shrewdness and openness match
Lois's. (Certainly that's how I felt when I interviewed him later
about his year's work.)

Time for one more example: from a quiet seaside resort in
Devon. This time teachers in the department had been actively joining in a regional workshop on approaches to literature. They had
tried out acting through a selected scene and discussing what they
wanted to communicate. Back in school, this is part of what Pauline
wrote after a similar experience. What is she learning from reading—
and from acting out—that scene in *The Winter's Tale* where Camillo
has to decide whether to obey his master, Leontes, and assassinate
one of their oldest friends, Polixenes, or whether to disobey the
panic command of Leontes' insane jealousy?

Camillo already in the state room but slightly in the shadows
is thinking over what Leontes has asked him to do. He finds
it very difficult to believe that Hermione and Polixenes are
lovers.

He hears Polixenes and turns round very surprised at seeing
him but trying to act normally. Polixenes comes closer, Camillo
starts to fidget and move awkwardly. They greet each other and
Polixenes asks Camillo what could be wrong with the king as he

thinks he is out of favour with him, Camillo answering that he does not know but indicating that he does:

"I dare not know, my Lord."

But the guilt shows in his face and Polixenes notices this. So Camillo must have sufficient expression to convey guilt.

Polixenes becomes angry and strolls angrily towards the audience almost appealing to them, how could Camillo not tell him but then he turns back when he says,

"Good Camillo,"

and becomes pleading. He says he (Camillo) must be a part in this because he sees Camillo's changed complexion and that tells him he must also have changed.

Camillo answers like a riddle probably breaking slightly away from Polixenes, saying it very softly but precisely, wishing to get it over with. He says that Polixenes has caused a sickness, which has made many ill but that he himself is totally oblivious of this. Camillo would then turn back and face Polixenes, who replies. He is shocked and confused, he does not understand and starts to walk and talk to the audience, but returning when he speaks directly to Camillo. Again he pleads with him to be more outspoken.

Camillo, by this time uncertain that he is doing the correct thing (after all Leontes trusts him), gives a weak answer and turns away from Polixenes.

Polixenes, totally tormented because he cannot think of what he has done, shakes Camillo,

"Dost thou hear, Camillo,"

then lets him go. He gesticulates with his arms towards the audience,

"How far off, how near . . . "

Camillo then very surprisingly says he will tell Polixenes. This is one of the difficulties because I think it is out of keeping with the scene and is awkward to place. Camillo must have been completely overcome by Polixenes' pleading and his honest appeal. So Camillo replies, "Since you have asked me in honour and I believe you to be honourable therefore listen to me. We must act swiftly or we will both be killed." At the end I think his relief would be obvious and the audience would feel the tension between the two men lift. Polixenes urges him on,

"On, good Camillo."

Camillo goes on to tell Polixenes everything that Leontes told him—convinced the king was wrong. I think Camillo put it delicately to Polixenes but still his reaction is very strong, he is shocked and stunned at Leontes' believing such lies about his friend.

Responses to Literature—What Is Being Assessed Vol. 2. John Dixon & John Brown, 1984/5, Schools Council Publications, distributed by NATE, U.K.

This is reading with an imaginative understanding beyond the words. Pauline is learning to interpret a complex text as clues to a pattern of feelings, attitudes and interaction as well as thoughts. To create these realistic images she has to think about how people behave under stress—when they feel suddenly shut out, or when they face a crucial order that goes against their better judgement. She is using what she knows of real people to turn the text into a "poem," as Louise Rosenblatt would say; to create an imaginative world in keeping with the words. In doing so, she realises this scene is about the breaking of one relationship and the making of another.

However, something more than that is happening, I believe. In communicating all this (and more) Pauline isn't speaking as student to teacher but as adult to equals. She has some confidence in explaining how to present this moment to others—and where the difficulties lie. It is this social relationship with the reader (or listener) that points to something vital for our ordinary students as they leave high school. Where will they stand in an adult world? What confidence will they have in their ability to learn, and to teach?

That key question seems to me inextricably linked to another: What is the quality of their teachers' confidence, *their* ability to teach—and *learn*? As it happens there is a sub-text behind all the classrooms I have drawn on, and many others I wished to include and celebrate here. All of those teachers have had the opportunity to work with colleagues in a local or national project. Many—if not all—have acted, written and read within project groups, learning by doing the things themselves that they ask students to do. All could try out ideas and expect understanding comments from colleagues whatever the relative achievements on a given day. All wanted to involve students across a range of abilities. All had some opportunity to consider *why* they might try these approaches and to look closely at what the students were achieving.

Some—but not as many as I would wish—also had the opportunity and incentive to report these things to a wider audience as I have done (and to learn in the process of doing so).

What are the lessons to be drawn? I believe that, through our associations, and internationally too, we have a case to make with parents, students, colleagues, and the public. That case is about the abilities not of exceptional but of ordinary students—given the right opportunities. But the basis for students' achievements lies with the opportunities given their teachers.

When I look back forty years at my teachers in school, I realise that they had no incentive or opportunity beyond individual idealism to learn about teaching English. After graduation they were not required to take a course in English Education. There was no national association to turn to for support. No national or local projects. No English consultants or other resources for in-service. Just one small journal, run on a shoe-string and selling perhaps a thousand copies or so.

By comparison today, the need for life-long professional education is just as real in teaching as it is in medicine. Personally, I have probably learnt more in the last five years than in the previous thirty —and almost all of it through discussion with colleagues.

So I believe we face two challenges: the first is to explore *all* the channels that exist to publicise what ordinary students can achieve, and to involve students alongside us in that campaign. The second is to win recognition for the professional rights of teachers, through associations like ours, to organise forms of continuing education that will affect the quality of our confidence, both as teachers and learners.

I do not imagine that will be easy. Many of those with political power are amazingly—and in some cases wilfully—ignorant of the range of positive work I have just begun to sample today. Many of those lower down the echelons—in Education itself—are looking for easy answers: they want to jack up standards by the routine application of graded or standardised tests. Their naivete shows in the terms they abuse: "measurement," "tested abilities," "skills" and so on. None of my evidence today comes from tests, and none is ever likely to.

For those who confuse "measurement" with "judgement" I would say this:

It is . . . never possible to arrive at a precise objective *measurement* of success in a piece of English work; attempts to do so usually concentrate on obvious surface features and ignore more important and complex elements. Assessment of work in

English is not a matter of precise measurement, or, usually, of simply marking things as right or wrong. It is a matter of the application of judgement, based on experience and knowledge of what to look for and an awareness of the whole as well as the parts. It is subjective; but subjective judgements based on professional knowledge and experience and clearly stated criteria are far preferable to the spurious objectivity of assessing the few aspects of English work that can be mechanically marked and ignoring the far more important ones that cannot.

English from 5 to 16. Department of Education & Science, 1984, Her Majesty's Stationery Office, U.K.

I take this perfectly common-sense, revolutionary statement from that hot-bed of subversion, Mrs. Thatcher's Department of Education and Science. (It has already been endorsed and commended by her Minister.)

Standards which depend on complex professional judgements can be upheld only by teachers who have internalised them and made them real in their own classrooms. This may be an ambitious project for mankind, but is it any less relevant than putting a man on the moon?

To my American friends I have to say: you may be members of "a nation at risk," but as a European I have to point out that for many of us it is the human species that is at risk today. It will take all our joint human understanding, common purpose, and determination to face those who play with that inhuman possibility. It is not a bad time to campaign for the humanities, if we can make the work deserve the term. And by such a positive campaign at this moment, we can at least offer the students of 1984 some modicum of hope for the social order of their future.

Language, Literature, and Values

LOUISE M. ROSENBLATT

New York University (U.S.A.)

To be alive is to make choices. Sometimes the choice is easy—
to jump out of the way of an oncoming car requires no deliberation.
The choice can be described as demonstrating a preference for the
value, life, as against death. In a stable, simple culture, most activities
would be guided by such automatic choices or value judgments. Our
values would mainly be those absorbed from the dominant value system of our cultural or social environment—from family, peer group,
"the media," school, community.

But in much of our lives today, many of the decisions we must
make cannot be automatic, nor can there be such clear choices between positive and negative values. The choice must often be made
between alternative positive values, between alternative goods. Should
I take the career that pays more or the more interesting one? Which
do I place higher, the values, *comfort* and *security*, or the values,
stimulation and *challenge*? Or in a classroom, how much of the values
of *order* and *quiet* must I be willing to give up in order to achieve the
values, *pupil initiative* or *creativity*? Even in a relatively stable society,
such choices between positive values must be made in decisions about
social and economic policies. A weighing of values, a sense of priorities in each situation becomes necessary.

In our present-day world of rapid social, economic, and cultural
change, reflection on our guiding values becomes even more essential.
Changes in economic processes, in family life, in relations between
the generations, in the roles of men and women, militate against
ready-made automatic decisions. The habitual choice may no longer
fit the new conditions. In a world beset by unprecedented threats of
poverty, pollution, and war, ready-made, unthinking responses are
anachronisms at least, and perhaps suicidal.

Because values have to do with the underlying dynamics or mo-
tivations in the life of individuals and societies, the term "values" has

64

been given varied definitions. Basic, it seems to me, is the idea that "value" points to that quality of anything which makes it, consciously or unconsciously, desired or preferred. In many contexts, we use the term simply in this way. But I should like to suggest, especially when I refer to reflection on choices in values, that the term "values" may also include not only what is desired, but also what is deemed worthy of being desired, what is desirable. The aim, in any educational or maturing process, should be the development of the capacity to arrive at such a considered sense of values.

Ability to reflect on questions of values becomes, then, an important part of our equipment for life. We need to learn to look beneath the stated surface values or aims to the actual values being affirmed by our own or others' decisions and actions. And beyond that, in the many areas of our lives in which old patterns are disintegrating, we need to reflect on our priorities. If there is to be a constructive decision, it must be appropriate to the total situation. It must be related to the individual's other value judgments and contribute to an understanding of what is essential to a humane way of life.

Surely, of all the arts, literature is most immediately implicated with life itself. The very medium through which the author shapes the text—language—is grounded in the shared lives of human beings. Language is the bloodstream of a common culture, a common history. What might otherwise be mere vibrations in the air or black marks on a page can point to all that has been thought or imagined— in Henry James' phrases, to "all life, all feeling, all observation, all vision."

Hence, literary works inevitably embody values: the simplest lyric affirms the importance of, places value on, some feelings, some experience, some person, some aspect of the world. Fiction—story, novel, drama—deals with human beings in situations in which they must make choices—and by those choices affirms the greater importance of one value over another. As Aristotle said, "character is that which reveals moral purpose, showing what kind of things a man chooses or avoids." Neither fantasy nor realism can escape the affirmation of some values and, even if only by implication, the rejection of others.

The Influence of Literature

The critical or historical analyst has largely been content to uncover the values accepted or rejected by characters within the work, or by the author through the medium of the text, and perhaps to suggest a personal judgment. The assumption has mainly been that this pattern of values will be absorbed by readers much as values are unconsciously absorbed from other parts of the social environment. When the influence of literature has been conceived in more active terms, it has often been viewed as providing models of behavior or, in more recent terminology, "role models." Reports on censorship and treatment of dissident authors throughout the world, such as the *Index of Censorship* compiles, testify to how much some governments believe, or fear, that literature does indeed have this power to influence behavior directly. No consensus on the nature and extent of such influence of literature exists.

The historical evidence is too complex for treatment here. We know that at any given time, literary works present a range of potential influences—some reflect the dominant values, others diverge from them. We know that works like *Uncle Tom's Cabin* and Koestler's *Darkness at Noon* have had political repercussions. We know, too, that there exists evidence such as John Stuart Mill's account of the psychological effects on him of the reading of Marmontel's memoirs and Wordsworth's poems. We know that psychological studies of the influence of fiction on social attitudes and behavior have not yielded consistent results. Interesting though it would be, I do not propose to engage in assessment of the social or personal impact of literature or the psychological, social or historical conditions that favor or deter such potential influence. I shall limit myself to, first, the question of how readers apprehend values in their evocation of literary works of art, and second, how the teaching of literature can foster the student's ability to reflect on issues in values.

My thesis will be that literature, when read *as* literature, is particularly adapted to providing the opportunity for fostering the ability to think rationally about values. But why not leave this concern to the social scientists, the historians, the guidance counselors? I agree that they, and indeed the whole school community, have an important responsibility in the moral development of our youth, since the home and other social institutions cannot be counted on alone to perform this function. I base my thesis that literature has a special role to play on two considerations: first, literary texts inevitably offer potential insights into values. Second, in evoking a literary work from a text the reader carries on a kind of activity that differs from the process required for reading natural or social science texts. This makes possible the special contribution of the literature classroom. In order to demonstrate this, I shall have to interpret the interrelationships of the three concepts contained in my title, and present a brief overview of my transactional theory of reading.

Language and Reading as Transaction

Even those who in recent years have discovered the importance of the reader's response have often seemed to assume that the response was to a work "out there," separate from the reader, somehow inhabiting the text alone. My transactional view of the reading process affirms that a literary work happens in the reciprocal relationship between reader and text. I term this relationship a "transaction" in order to emphasize the fluid, dynamic circuit, a to-and-fro process over time, the interfusion of reader and text in a unique synthesis that constitutes "the meaning," whether it happens to be a scientific report or a poem.

"Transaction" underlines my rejection of the epistemological dualism that would place the human being over against nature as two separate or autonomous entities. Current ecological views of the human being in a two-way relationship with nature, and current philoophy of science, with its recognition of the observer as an explicit factor in any observation or proposition, illustrate the transactional concept. John Dewey (1896) reacted early against the stimulus-response view of the organism passively receiving the stimulus, and showed that the organism in a sense seeks out or modifies the stimuli to which it responds. As "interaction" suggested the dualism which he had long opposed, Dewey, in *Knowing and the Known* (1949) chose the term "transaction" to indicate a two-way, reciprocal relationship; thus "knowing" assumes a transaction between a knower and a known.

"Transaction" seems especially to be needed for a description of the act of reading. Reading is always a particular event, involving a particular reader, a particular item of the environment—a text—at a particular time, under particular circumstances. A person becomes a reader by virtue of a relationship with a text. A text is merely ink on paper, until some reader, if only the author,* evokes meaning from it. The transactional theory resists the formalist tendency to concentrate on the text as all-important and the reader as passive, and also avoids the alternative extremism of some recent "subjective" literary theorists who see the reader as all-important and the text as passive or secondary. Reader and text are mutually essential to the transaction; meaning happens during the transaction between the reader and the text.

---

*The author's text emerges from a personal and social transaction, but as the reader encounters only the text, we can deal here primarily with the reading act, through which "communication" takes place.

The reader's give and take with the text reflects the transactional nature of all language. Language is socially generated and socially acquired, a public system of communication. In contemporary jargon, language is never to be understood as context independent. But it is easily forgotten that language is always individually internalized. It is essential to conceptualize the processes by which the individual participates in the public language system.

My view of language stems ultimately from William James (1890) and C. S. Peirce (1932). James's brilliant metaphor of the stream of thought or consciousness (which now typically serves as a point of departure for cognitive psychologists emerging from the behaviorist interlude) encompasses not only ideas but "every form of consciousness"—sensations, images, percepts and concepts, states or qualities of states, feelings of relations, feelings of tendency. As we think of the objects our words point to or of the relationships among them, our stream of consciousness matches each of them by an inward coloring of its own.

C. S. Peirce's triadic formulation for the linguistic symbol provides for the transaction between the individual and the environment. "The sign," Peirce wrote, "is related to its object only in consequence of a mental association, and depends upon habit." The psychologists' phrasing for this (e.g. Werner and Kaplan, 1963; Bates, 1979) is that a word acquires meaning when the word and its referent are linked to the same inner organismic state. Vygotsky (1962) points out that in contrast to the dictionary meaning of a word, its "sense" is "the sum of all the psychological events aroused in our consciousness by the word. It is a dynamic, fluid, complex whole." For the young child, the word "cat" is as much an attribute of the creature as its fur or its pointed ears. The child learns to "decontextualize" the word, to sort out its external reference to a class, but this rests, as Vygotsky reminds us, on a personal, experiential base.

This personal linguistic reservoir of cognitive, kinaesthetic and affective elements is built up around words through our specific past experiences with life and language. This is all that the reader (and, let me add, the writer, the speaker, the listener) has to draw on. From this, we create the new meaning, the new experience, that the transaction with the text makes possible.

Selective Attention in Reading

Given the view of language much too briefly sketched thus far, it becomes possible to look more closely at the reading process. The reader brings to the text the internalized "sum," the accumulation or memory, of past "organismic" encounters with language and the world. In reading, the words of the text may be said to transact with elements of memory, to stir up the organismic states linked to the words—states which encompass not only the public referents or objects to which the verbal symbols point, but also the personal aspects —sensuous, affective, imaginal and associative. Thus the evocation of meaning from the text requires a selecting-out from the reservoir of thought and feeling. "Selective attention" is William James's (1890) name for this acceptance of some elements into the center of attention and relegation of others to the periphery of awareness.

Reading thus consists in a continuing flow of selective synthesis on the reader's part. There is the need to develop guides for the selective process, guides that set up expectations and hence narrow the range of options from which to choose. Just as in the sequence of verbal symbols the article "a" suggests the syntactic category from which to choose the meaning of the next word, so the reader seeks cues to the formation of a guiding semantic principle—tentative, open to constant revision—that will direct the process of selective attention. If expectations are inappropriate to subsequent verbal symbols in the text, revision of the guiding principle of selection, or perhaps a complete rereading, occurs. Selective attention thus serves the choosing, structuring, synthesizing activity which produces meaning.

The Efferent and the Aesthetic Stance

The most decisive act of selective attention still remains to be defined. The general intention to make meaning out of the verbal symbols, though necessary, is not sufficient for a fully successful reading. The *kind* of meaning must be delimited. Either before the encounter with the text, or early in the reading event, the reader must select a general stance, a mental set, toward the internal states that will be activated by the pattern of words.

Every linguistic act, we have seen, consists of both public and private elements—the general terms I have used to include aspects variously referred to as cognitive and affective, referential and emotive, denotative and connotative. The reader must choose the purpose, the mental set, that will determine the relative degrees of attention to be bestowed on the public and private aspects of the field of consciousness activated by the words. I term this the reader's choice of a predominant "stance." This will direct the whole selective process.

One part of the continuum of potential stances covers the mental set that I term the "efferent" stance, from the Latin *effere*, "to carry away." In such reading, attention is focussed mainly on building the public meaning that is to be carried away from the reading: actions to be performed, information to be retained, conclusions to be drawn, solutions to be arrived at, analytic concepts to be applied, propositions to be tested. Such a stance usually dominates the reading of a textbook, a cooking recipe, a scientific report. The personal, sensuous, associative elements of consciousness are subordinated or ignored.

In contrast to the efferent focus of attention on what is to be retained *after* the reading, in the predominantly aesthetic stance, the reader focuses attention primarily on what is being lived through *during* the reading. The span of attention opens out to attend not only to the public referents for the verbal symbols, but also to what we are seeing and feeling and thinking, on what is aroused within us by the very sound of the words, and by what they point to in the human and natural world. *The new experience that we shape out of these elements, through a process of selection and synthesis, is for us the poem or story or play.* Moreover, we respond to the very literary work that we are creating under guidance of the text.

Every reading act falls somewhere on the continuum between the efferent and the aesthetic poles. Most readings probably fall somewhere near the middle of the continuum, i.e., attention covers both public and private areas of consciousness that are resonating to the words, but in different proportions, according to the reader's purpose.

In predominantly efferent reading, as in, for example, the reading of a book about ecology, the cumulation of information would be the predominant interest, but some associative, affective elements might appropriately be admitted into the range of attention. Similarly, in predominantly aesthetic reading, there is always an efferent referential component but attention centers on the spectrum of feelings, sensations, associations, ideas, in which the referential meanings are embedded.

Note that "efferent" and "aesthetic" refer to the reader's stance and not to the text. No matter what the intentions of the author or the linguistic potentialities of the text, any text can be read either efferently or aesthetically. A reader's purpose toward the same text may vary. Even when we have honored the lyric poet's intention, the same text can be read efferently, if only its "literal" meaning is desired; or a novel can be analyzed efferently as a social document. And it is a cliché to speak of the mathematician who looks at his solution aesthetically and admires its "elegance."

Unfortunately, traditional teaching of reading has failed to do justice to the need to adopt either the aesthetic or the efferent as the *predominant* stance. Much reading seems muddled or counter-productive at present because of the reader's confusion about stance. Thus a political statement may be read with too much dominance given to the affective, associative elements, when the reader's purpose presumably should be to discover verifiable reasons for, say, what taxation policies should be adopted. Much reading of advertisements fits that pattern. Even more pervasive is the efferent reading of texts of stories, poems, plays, with the consequent loss of their essential experiential qualities and values as works of art.

The Efferent Bias in Teaching

The false assumption that the text dictates the reader's stance has unfortunately resulted in a concern mainly with the question of what texts to present to students and with the inculcation of an accepted interpretation. There has been little or no help given in differentiating the appropriate stance for an aesthetic reading. An inordinate overemphasis on the efferent has been the consequence. Our technologically oriented, mainly extrovert culture has favored language in its public, impersonal, instrumental, scientific manifestations. The teaching of reading in the schools has been based mainly on efferent models of the reading process. Preoccupation with methods of inculcating the "skills," essential though that may be, has centered almost entirely on the cognitive, informative aspects of reading. The aesthetic (or "literary") has been considered, if at all, as a variation on the efferent process, requiring only the addition to it of new skills or "strategies," not a different stance.

The basic teaching problem was epitomized for me years ago by a third-grade reading workbook. A page with broad margins and uneven lines of print announced the text of a poem. Above the title, however, appeared the question: "What facts does this poem teach you?" That question taught the pupils that one approaches a poem just as one approaches an informative text, efferently seeking the answers to be given at the end of the reading. Basal reading texts and their teachers' manuals manifest the same partiality: stories and poems, introduced because of the young child's obvious interest, are nevertheless surrounded by the same kinds of questions and comments as would apply to a purely informative text.

When, in the later school years, the curriculum includes the "study of literature," usually the approach is still primarily efferent, with the students demonstrating "comprehension" by reporting their memory of details and recounting the sequence of ideas or events. A similar approach prevails as they move into high school and college. Even when students achieve an aesthetic experience, they are often hurried away from it to efferent concerns, paraphrases, analyses, proofs that they have read the text, that they have "understood" it (efferently). No wonder that those who want to change the emphasis and introduce a "response" approach often at first meet silence, suspicion, or superficiality. The students have been exposed to "literary" texts, year after year, but they typically have not learned how to produce a truly literary experience or to pay attention to their own responses.

Experiencing Tensions in Values

The reader, we have seen, needs to approach the text with an aesthetic stance, prepared to allow into the center of attention not only the ideas but also the attendant attitudes, sensations, feelings, and overtones that are stirred up and that can be structured into the evocation, the literary work. And there will be the stream of concurrent reactions to the emerging work to ponder and build on. Instead of being hurried away from this experience into efferent analytic activities, the young reader needs to be encouraged, first of all, to savor the evocation, to recapture its quality, to recall the stream of reactions—what captured the interest, what seemed important, what stirred, what pleased or displeased, what puzzled or enlightened, what answered questions or raised them. No matter how incomplete or inadequate the evocation may be in comparison with the teacher's transaction, this is "the work" for the student, and, as current learning theory tells us, such personal experience provides the roots for growth in the capacity to transact more adequately with literary texts. This does not imply that "anything goes," but rather rests on the assumptions that growth builds on and extends already-acquired powers—and also that growth in reading abilities happens best in a meaningful context. I shall later return to suggest how a collaborative classroom atmosphere may lead to self-awareness and self-criticism, both in the area of reading process and in clarification of issues in values.

The writings of philosophers and social scientists can tell us *about* issues in values, can formulate hypothetical problems, can provide theoretical scaffoldings for consideration of alternatives. But young people may not have the life experience required to give substance to abstract statements of problems in values, and this may lead to superficial interpretations. Yet thinking about choices in values as they are confronted in actual life may be equally flawed, distorted by strong emotions and the pressure of value systems unquestioningly absorbed from a narrow environment. Literary texts, when they are part of an aesthetic transaction, afford direct experience, but with sufficient distance for reflection. As Solzhenitsyn said in his Nobel Prize lecture (1972), art and literature can perform a miracle: "they can overcome man's unfortunate trait of learning only through his own experience. . . . recreating in the flesh what another has experienced, and allowing it to be acquired as one's own."

Recently, I reread William Faulkner's story "Barn Burning." You may recall the nine-year-old boy's anguish at his bitter sharecropper father's vengefully setting fire to rich landowners' barns. I suffered with the boy, "pulled two ways like between two teams of horses": the painful tensions between a child's identification with his father—his impulse to "stick to your own blood"—and the sense of something else being important. Faulkner tells us that twenty years later the boy was to name the values that as a child he had already understood—"truth, justice." Having shared the intense conflict in values, I found myself pondering not only the boy's decision, but also the values of the author and of the divided society he had enabled me to enter. And I found that even from my own adult angle of vision, I was having to differentiate between understanding the unfortunate causes of violent behavior, and recognizing the values that prevented my condoning it.

Another illustration: many have "studied" Joyce's *A Portrait of the Artist as a Young Man* as a document in Joyce's biography, as an illustration of innovation in techniques of fiction, as a commentary on life in Ireland. The young reader especially responds to the end of the work: Stephen has emancipated himself from childhood ties and goes forth to discover his own identity—"to forge in the smithy of [his] soul the uncreated conscience of [his] race." If they do indeed enter into the work and are not simply led to read it to identify theme, symbol, and point of view, they join Stephen in his adolescent trying-on of one role after another. They remember more than the final rejection. They share with him the tension between positive values—the appeal of the order and mystery and power of the church and the appeal of the fullblooded life of the senses and the imagination—and between the camaraderie of his nationalist fellow-students and his desire to be free of all circumscribing allegiances. He must choose between things that have positive value for him; he must decide what is most important for one of his temperament and talents.

The book thus has excited in young readers reflection on the kinds of choices open to individuals in relation to family, friends, and society. It has led to reflection on the different bases for choice appropriate to different temperaments and life styles. It has led to both acceptance and challenge of the values of the alienated artist and has fostered an awareness of identity even for those of very different temperament in very different social situations. Study of the work as a document in the life of its author or as a landmark in literary history can be a secondary activity.

The unique potentialities of this and other texts to illuminate values derive precisely from the fact that in the aesthetic or literary transaction the reader lives through the work "in the flesh." The reader is freed from the emotional wrenchings of choices in "real life," yet, drawing on a personal reservoir of ideas and feelings, participates directly in the tensions in values embodied in the literary evocation. As we call forth a work we face the necessity for choices. We may identify with the persona of a lyric, so that the words seem an emanation of our own emotions. In a story or novel, we may share in the characters' predicaments, strain with them toward one or another value. We can suffer or enjoy the human consequence of different choices in values. We may be pleased or puzzled or angered at those choices. In transaction with texts, we may transcend our own limitations of gender, age, temperament, environment, place, or time, to discover undreamed-of affirmations of, or distinctions in, values. We may participate in whole societies of men and women living by values very different from our own, and we may be helped to sense more keenly the structured human meanings of our own society.

Reflection in an Emotional Context

Emphasis on literary experience is sometimes misunderstood as simply the equating of the aesthetic with emotion. Good and great writers have given us ample evidence that emotion and reason are not opposed. Cognition is always accompanied by some affective elements, and emotion is *about* something cognized. John Dewey (1922) pointed out, "Rationality . . . is not a force to evoke against impulse and habit. It is the attainment of a working harmony among diverse desires." If I have found it necessary to underline the necessity for the aesthetic stance, it is not simply because the literary work helps readers to become aware of problems in values that are part of the human condition, and to become cognizant of alternative sets of values. Even more important, a literary experience, an aesthetic reading, can help us approximate toward the orchestration of values, the handling of impulse, emotion and thought, out of which rationality may emerge.

Priorities in the Classroom

The literature classroom which is unconcerned with the experiential evocation of the literary work teaches students that the significant values in the reading of literature are the efferent retention of such matters as the "facts" of the plot of a novel, its classification as, say, a novel of manners, its narrative methods, or its place in literary history. Poems are to be read, in such classes, in order, for example, to efferently state their literal "meaning," to categorize their genres, or to analyze their metaphors and verse forms. The notion that "literariness" resides entirely in such formal aspects leads also to concentration on teaching critical terminology.

An instance of the dominance of such formalistic values was recounted recently, in an article in the *New Republic* (April 2, 1984) on the critical history of a poem by the German poet, Paul Celan. After the brutal murder of his parents in a Nazi concentration camp, and his own narrow escape from such a fate, Celan wrote a poem based on an actual happening: a Nazi officer in a concentration camp had forced Jewish musicians to play a tango while their fellow prisoners dug their own graves. The poet speaks for such victims in a complex web of narrative, lyric, and satiric elements, first entitled *Todestango* (Deathtango) and published in 1948 as *Todesfuge* (Deathfugue). We are told: *Todesfuge*

> was ensconced in anthologies during the '50s and, notably, in high school readers. Students would spend a few preliminary minutes on "content preparation," then go on assiduously to analyze the poem's prosody and structure. Having studied fugues in music class, they might each adopt a motif or voice to perform Celan's poem, "to make the polyphony audible"— with what effect, it's hard to know. One pedagogical journal does advise giving the class something historical first (but not about genocide—better Anne Frank's Diary). And "the point is for this to happen before interpreting *Todesfuge*" . . . because "a consideration of *Todesfuge* could easily lapse into discussion of the persecution of the Jews."

This treatment of Celan's work carried to a logical extreme the belief that the responsibility of the classroom is primarily to the formal aspects of literature. For Celan's compatriots, such formalist analysis undoubtedly provided an evasion of the guilt of a recent ugly past. Can it be that, without such powerful provocation, in many of our English-speaking classrooms an efferent preoccupation with formalist values offers a similar comfortable escape from moral complexities?

Ironically, questions of form and technique are actually highly relevant to Celan's poem. Its fugal form, its driving repetitions, its ironic allusions, and its gripping metaphors, are noteworthy. However, they should be pondered on, not as an evasion of the poem's human meaning, but as an aspect of that experienced meaning. A classroom that values, above all, the personal, human significance of the literary experience need not ignore, but will naturally move on to consider such formal literary values. They will come to be seen, not as ends or values in themselves, but as values indissolubly linked with the human import of the literary experience.

The Aesthetic Basis for Value Judgment

No matter how much students are exposed to the texts of the good and great works that are our heritage, literature will survive only if our literature classrooms have as their first priority engendered in students the capacity for aesthetic reading, as the basis for the habit of reflection on the personal and social impact of literary works. More is implied here than simply the avoidance of overemphasis on matters of form, biography, or literary history. Positive efforts are needed to encourage the aesthetic reading of literary texts for personal pleasure and enriched experience. This requires a classroom atmosphere that furthers participation in the world of the work. Young readers need to be helped to develop habits of attention to the broad spectrum of sound, sense, imagery, and feeling that color the ideas and events as they are being shaped into a poem or a story. Pupils should feel free, also, to pay attention to their own reactions, as the imagined world confirms, or collides with, their own prior lives and convictions. The task of the classroom then is to help the young reader to organize and interpret this experience. Opportunities for spontaneous expression should be provided. Instead of hurrying the student away into extrinsic analytic concerns, the teacher can lead the young reader back to savor, to recollect, to reenact, at least in imagination, the experienced work and the reactions that accompanied it. Such deepening and ordering of the experience can be spurred by open-ended questions or opportunities for nonverbal as well as verbal responses.

Collaborative Teaching and Learning

The teaching of literature in these circumstances becomes something different from the imparting or imposition of the teacher's (or some critical authority's) interpretation of the texts. It makes enhanced reading "skills" a by-product of meaningful reading and discussion, and not an end in itself. The teaching-learning relationship is collaborative, with the students seeking to relate their varied evocations and responses to the elements or aspects of the text that triggered or support them. Out of such sharing and interchange can come self-awareness, self-criticism, and hence enhanced capacity to

handle the intellectual and emotional activities that constitute transactions with literary texts.

My purpose is not to deny the values to be found in traditional
literary criticism or literary history, but to clarify priorities. Critical
activities and insights are hollow verbalizations if they do not spring
from, center on, and illuminate personally shaped literary experiences. The literature classroom must first, we have said, create the
environment for participation—the direct personal entrance into the
expanded world made possible by transactions with literary texts.
From such participation in the work will flow reflection on the
gamut of emotions, roles, situations, ideas lived through. Concern
with values does not require morals to be drawn or "messages" to be
formulated. The teacher will not impose an interpretation or a judgment, but critical standards will be collaboratively developed, reject-
ing the notion that "anything goes," and finding in the text the
means for communicating with one another about the necessarily
individual transactions between each reader and that text.

The group will be stimulated to look more closely at the text
in order to mediate among different interpretations and judgments.
They should try to understand what values are affirmed or rejected
by their own reactions. They should become aware of how the attitudes they brought to the text differ from the values dominant in
the world of the work, or how their own values have been illuminated, reinforced or modified by the literary experience. In short,
they should develop the habit of thinking rationally about things
that engage their emotions. The feeling that what each reader makes
of the text merits consideration makes for increased understanding
and self-criticism. Through interchange, readers often discover their
strengths and weaknesses, their sensitivities and blind spots. Literary
experience becomes one among many kinds of experience, offering
the possibility of responsible acceptance or rejection—the discarding
of what is anachronistic and the assimilation of what is nourishing
for human beings living in this age of appalling dangers and dazzling
possibilities. The teaching of literature becomes, then, not the inculcation of a rigid set of priorities or hierarchy of values, but the pro-
vision of opportunities for the development of habits of thoughtful
discrimination and judgment concerning emotionally-laden choices
in values.

Relativism and Affirmation

This view of literature teaching should not be confused with an
extreme, negativistic relativism. The over-simplified conception of
scientific "truth" and the impersonality of so-called objective

criticism concerned only with formal traits of the literary work have reinforced the school's abdication of its role in fostering the assimilation of socially desirable habits of thought and action. This educational vacuum offers no protection from the forces leading to the—often asocial—alienation of so many of our youth. This question is fundamental for our whole educational system, and the answers we find for the teaching of literature have implications for not only other aspects of language education, but for the whole educational and social process.

No human situation, and hence no school or classroom situation, can avoid imparting, affirming, some set of values. Since values are always assimilated in concrete situations, refusal to indoctrinate a set of values does not spell complete neutrality, because that is not humanly possible. Teachers need to bring their own motivating values into consciousness, and to scrutinize the values they are tacitly indoctrinating through their teaching methods and their personal attitudes. (The parallel question of the values built into the character of the whole school community and its administrative structure is treated in other sections of this volume.) When the teacher is involved in a collaborative relationship with students, working together with them to clarify the problems in interpretation presented by a text, the teacher can feel freer to express personal value judgments without fear of being accused of indoctrination.

We can avoid rigid indoctrination, we can be pluralists, we can encourage consideration of alternative systems of value, yet accept our responsibility to promote the individual reader's search for a personal sense of priorities that will guide sound choices in values in a changing world. The transactional theory of reading and the view of the literature classroom presented here insist on the essential role of the reader; this honoring of the individual student is consonant with belief in the fundamental value of the individual human being, the keystone value that we in the English-speaking countries share. Human beings are recognized as having inherent value: anything which reduces them to the status of things, instruments, or automata is condemned. And since the individual is such by virtue of transactions with other individuals in social groups, the aim of the greatest possible well-being and fulfillment of individual humans brings with it the corollary that this cannot be achieved at the expense of the dehumanization of others. Weighing the consequences of any social arrangement or moral code for actual human lives becomes, then, the basis of value judgment.

The very freedom of thought and speech that we offer the student derives from the underlying valuation placed on the individual, and we should have no hesitancy in making this implicit democratic value the explicit foundation on which the child or youth can build a personal sense or hierarchy of priorities. This makes it possible to compare the values absorbed from the immediate environment with the values expressed in other social arrangements or attitudes.

Such critical reflection on values need not be merely negative. Youth's confusion and sense of futility often result from awareness of injustice and inadequacy in our world without any clearly felt emotional drive toward the creation of more humanly satisfying and humanistic ways of life. Literary experience, precisely because it involves the whole person, drawing on both cognitive and affective aspects of consciousness, can illuminate values worthy of fulfillment and can help to generate the emotional drive to achieve those values.

Auden, in his "In Memory of W. B. Yeats," tells us that "poetry makes nothing happen," thus denying the Victorian notion of the didactic and moralistic effect of literature. But he reinforces our transactional views when he goes on to say, "It is a way of happening," and when he reminds us that "The words of a dead man/Are modified in the guts of the living." Even as the poet enables us to suffer the lack of humane values in our world, he is enabling us to affirm their importance. There is no contradiction, then, when he ends his elegy with an affirmative image of the poet's role.

> In the deserts of the heart
> Let the healing fountains start,
> In the prison of his days
> Teach the free man how to praise.

REFERENCES

Bates, E. (1979). *The Emergence of Symbols.* New York: Acedemic Press.

Dewey, J. (1896). The reflex arc concept in psychology. *Psychological Review, 3,* 357–70. (Reprinted as "The Unit of Behavior" in *Philosophy and Civilization.* New York: Capricorn, 1963.)

Dewey, J. (1922). *Human Nature and Conduct.* New York: Henry Holt.

Dewey, J., & Bentley, A. F. (1949). *Knowing and the Known.* Boston: Beacon Press.

James, H. (1888). *Partial Portraits.* London: Macmillan.

James, W. (1890). *The Principles of Psychology.* Vol. I. New York: Henry Holt.

Peirce, C. S. (1932). *Collected Works.* Vol. 2. Cambridge, MA: Harvard University Press.

Solzhenitsyn, A. (1972). *Nobel Lecture.* New York: Farrar, Straus and Giroux.

Vygotsky, L. S. (1962). *Thought and Language.* Cambridge: M.I.T. Press.

Werner, H. & Kaplan, B. (1963). *Symbol and Formation.* New York: Wiley.

Language, Schooling, and Teacher Education

MARY MAGUIRE
McGill University (Canada)

Let us recognize that tacit knowing is the fundamental power of the mind, which creates explicit knowing, lends meaning to it and controls its uses. . . .

Michael Polanyi

Michael Polanyi, the influential philosopher, physical chemist and social scientist, argues that people have the capacity to acquire knowledge even though they cannot always specify the grounds on which they know, and to produce discoveries by steps they cannot always specify. What meanings do Polanyi's ideas have for those of us who work in education and are concerned about language, learning, schooling and society? One of the challenges implied by this question is an interpretative one. What is teacher education? One of the problems is a conflict between what the university academics of the varied disciplines which funnel into teacher education programmes think it is and should be and what the professionals who work in schools know it to be and or hope it can be.

In this paper I argue that

—the fragmentation, neologism, and scientific obscurantism which Polanyi asserts have pervaded our universe and distorted scientific inquiry, underlie much professional thought in education about teaching and learning generally and more specifically distort the goals of education theory, research and practice;
—the nature of knowing and human learning as far as teachers are concerned cannot be separated from their personal participation in the learning process nor from the experiences of their students coming to know;
—the essence of teacher education, human learning for that matter at all levels, is how to make people—teachers and students—aware of their own meanings and the meanings of others;

81

—this tacit process of knowing for all human beings is a continuous, living, dynamic process of social construction of reality.

However, our present teacher education programmes and *schooling in general* at all levels work against these central notions of tacit knowing, knowing as a living and dialogic process. As I reflect back on the history of educational research (from my own personal parsing of courses and schooling), I see too clearly an image of a checkered history of chi squaredom and a surfeit of anti-educational ways of linear thinking not only embedded in our research paradigms but in the very language of such research.

As I read John Goodlad's new book, *A Place Called School,* I kept thinking that the prospects for the future of teacher education indeed look grim; out of a massive, impressive 376-page chronicle scrutinizing North American schools from varied perspectives, Goodlad devotes seven pages to the subject of teacher education. While in retrospect I think he tells a better story of schooling than Michael Rutter does in his *Fifteen Thousand Hours* which ends with a well-timed punchline that "schools matter," I continue to be more intrigued by two leitmotifs which run throughout the Goodlad text: 1. ours is a much schooled society; 2. people go to school as part of growing up—suggesting that "people matter."

Because I believe that it is rather difficult, if not impossible to measure the intensity and depth of a learning experience by objective exercises, I want to offer three examples of anecdotal evidence to serve as signs signifying the values inherent in our present educational system:

Anecdotal Evidence One

Two years past I had occasion to observe a student teacher, fifteen years my senior. I recall how I arrived at the door of her classroom ahead of time, to be greeted by a noisy group of fifth graders huddled up like the old lady in the English ballad, barring the door to anyone who was not prepared to check their experience at the entrance.

To a young chap's query, *Are you a sub?* I replied, *No.* The pursuit of inquiry was on; questions followed in quick succession: *Why are you here? Are you the student teacher? No,* I replied, only to be further interrogated: *Well why are you here?* In retrospect, I recall mumbling *I'm here to learn about teaching.* My answer did not satiate his curiosity. I remember well his fervor and my own attempt to record the structure and organization of this student teacher's lesson, left eye fixated to the lines on my note pad, right eye focused on the lines of intensity etched on his young brow. As he inched his chair over to mine at the average rate of a centimetre per second, I recall how observation gave way to questioning as he whispered, *When you grow up, do you want to become a teacher?* Given that one of our central problems in teacher education in Quebec is our aged teaching population—the mean age of our working teachers is forty plus—I felt a little flattered that from this young chap's perception, I hadn't passed for a member of our Quebec teaching profession, seemingly lacking the salient genealogical features of the clan! But alas I remember Picasso—it takes a long time to become young; and I add a rejoinder—it takes a long time to understand.

My point here is that if we are really concerned with teachers and learners being active agents of their own inquiries, as this young chap is, then we must recognize a fundamental premise of human learning and of how the pursuit of scientific inquiry proceeds:

> The efforts of perception are induced by a craving to make out what it is that we are seeing before us. They respond to the conviction that we can make sense of experience, because it hangs together in itself. Scientific inquiry is motivated likewise by the craving to understand things. Such an endeavor can go on only if sustained by hope, the hope of making contact with the hidden pattern of things. . . . I believe that this commitment makes sense in view of man's position in the universe.
>
> (Polanyi, 1969, p. 120)

And my question is this: From your personal vantage point, from what you have experienced, learned and know now, if you were to start over, how many of you would answer the young boy affirmatively? I pose the question because in all our countries, I am certain that we can quickly garner a surfeit of stories that point to the fact that we, in teacher education, are indeed in *Hard Times*. The political and social assaults are not confined to our schools— although it is these structures which have been subject to the most intensive scrutiny. Under the rubric of effective schooling, the lives of the people who work in these places called schools are measured out not by "coffee spoons" but marked by "time on tasks." The sound of "Hurry up please it's time," resonates through the halls of schools, colleges, departments and faculties of education.

Anecdotal Evidence Two

Everyone knows that schools are linear; schooling is a linear process; everybody knows, to borrow a line from Eliot's Prufrock, "What and how to presume" about and in schools. In response to my question, How do you become a teacher?, eight-year-old Sarah offered the following explanation of the process of getting a teaching license:

> First you go to a building. You take some courses. You do a test on a school, in a school. You wear a square hat. They give you a degree. And then you can mess around with kids.

That our schools are so predictable, that teaching is such a rule-governed activity, is also evident from the attempt of a group of ten-year-olds to create their own entrepreneurial enterprise during the course of a summer vacation. After five years of experience writing "Summer Fun" stories which were by tradition the first day of school sent for holistic assessment to school board officials policing literacy standards in some of our inner city schools in Montreal, these six boys spent their creative energies generating model stories for their schoolmates in grades 1, 2, 3, 4 and 5 and sold them for a dime a copy. What is fascinating about their stories is their accuracy and sense of appropriate language use, which included spelling errors and printed and cursive variations in each collection of stories produced for each of the graded levels. Because schooling is so predictable and occurs in such linear fashion as these children show us, it is with predictable regularity attacked and satirized not only by adults who have experienced the system but also by children who are currently doing school.

Anecdotal Evidence Three

Excerpts from an *Autobiography* by T. S., grade five:

> It is the late afternoon of Sept. 15, 1972, when a baby was born at the Queen Elizabeth Hospital in Montreal. His Ukranian parents called him _____, which, in English, means T. S. He came into the world silent and happy, but that wouldn't last long. At the tender age of two, while being babysat, he was playing in the bathtub, unseen by his babysitter, a neighbor. He turned a few valves enjoying himself. As a result, the water gushed out of the spout, temporarily burning his feet. In a few months, his feet were okay, his feelings weren't. From that day

forward anything that was cold to anyone else would be very hot to T. . . .

When he was three, he went to a daycare center at the Hollefeur Chalet. His parents also sent him to Ukranian school for three hours every Saturday. He loved playing in nursery school, but he would hate the strenuous work from kindergarten to grade four. (He didn't go into grade five.)

Nothing eventful happened until he reached the ripe age of five. Then he started kindergarten at Larkwood Elementary School. His principal was Mr. J. and his teacher was Mrs. R. The boys in Mrs. R.'s class loved to make a building out of boxes and cylinders. After the building was high enough, they would remove two of the bottom cylinders, then making the building fall and collapse.

In grade one his teacher was Miss C., the music specialist. If her singing group sung the notes wrong, she used to warm them up by making them sing the scale backwards. Through Miss C., T's long wanted urge to read came true, and his reading group became famous in Miss C.'s record books. They overran the reading level for grade one, and they had to be given a novel to read in class!!

In grade two, he was in a mixed two/three class, in which his teacher was Mrs. G. He started in a so-so reading group, but he quickly rose to the second best reading group. (The best was just for grade three). He also started developing a *great* interest in books and he couldn't wait until library day. . . .

His grade three teacher, like his grade two teacher, was Mrs. G. This year, however, it was different. Mrs. G. gave out Creative Writing Assignments three times a month (hint, hint, Mrs. G.) and T. always came through with the most creative, most original and, of course, longest stories. This he loved doing, and that encouraged him to be a journalist. . . .

Lakewood school closed that year, but the memories wouldn't. Mrs. G. and a few other teachers were transferred to Beachcroft School, along with T. and half of the kids from Lakewood.

The next year he was completely different from the previous one, oh, sure, his love for books remained but he felt out of place. Beachcroft was *a lot* different from Lakewood.

Another thing that changed was the story writing. His English teacher, Mrs. H. gave very little story writing ideas, and the ones she gave weren't so hot anyway. T. didn't despair. Mrs. G. was at Beachcroft.

In grade five, T. thought that his story writing would get back into swing with Mrs. G. as his English teacher. They didn't. Mrs. G. didn't give out Creative Writing assignments for the last two terms. She was hung up on book reports. She gave Creative Writing assignments for the first two terms but T. wasn't interested in writing those kinds of stories.

T. didn't despair. He currently wants to be a lawyer, a musician and most importantly a journalist!

The end?

Mrs. G.'s comments:

This is quite an autobiography, full of interesting events which will no doubt mould a great writer. Perhaps, it is this piece of work which will get you back into that creative writing stream as we knew it in Grade two and three. Please respond to my note, if you haven't already done so, with your suggestions for creative writing assignments.

This piece suggests to me the significance of what *choices* teachers and students perceive they have in using the power of knowledge and language for observing, inquiring and creating, for becoming aware of their own meanings in their social construction of reality. Thus, this emphasis on the personal participation of knowers and knowing as a living process, inherent in Dixon's personal growth model, does not imply to me a retreat to irrational subjectivity which allows individuals to do as they please but rather assures them the right and provides them with opportunity to speak the truth as we know it and for those *who* listen, to recognize and accept it.

*   *   *

In a book entitled, *Human Brain and Human Learning*, Lester Hart makes the case that linear, fragmented instruction, a major argument in this paper, is brain antagonistic. He states that the brain is not organized nor designed for linear one-path thoughts but that

most electronic computers do work linearly. One step leading to the next (although most recent, sophisticated types give hints of not remaining quite so limited). But the brain operates by simultaneously going down many paths . . . Experienced teachers widely agree that the more different approaches they use the better the learning is apt to be, yet most yield to pressures for logic.

(Hart, 1983, p. 52)

If human learning is not a linear progression, why is it so in our very institutions which train our teachers and do educational research? Nowhere do I see the personal growth model of human learning as being more brain antagonist, in Hart's sense, than in our fragmented teacher education programmes, undergraduate and graduate. Our present preservice, inservice models of teacher education too readily discount the personal knowledge and experience teachers have and provide little if any opportunity to create knowledge for themselves —knowledge that is worked out and shared with others, to experience and realize the transforming power of what is learned. If we are talking about teacher education, we are talking about the epistemological basis of a learning community: that our students get to know what knowing is. I believe that too many are excellent at doing school, at mustering the nomenclature, neologisms, the courses and the credits and find little time nor volition to engage with or explore the meaning of their words and their influence on others.

I despair when I see young graduate students with one or two years experience of learning in classrooms *with children* take professional nomenclature and set up curriculum units of fragmented *transactional, expressive* and *poetic* learning situations for a graduate curriculum seminar and receive and "A." Our teacher education programmes must ensure that our students have opportunity to reflect back and to create a story of what they have learned or in a sense of what they have muddled through. Otherwise they will simply muddle through teaching—what they were told, how they were told it. We have in fragmenting schooling, language and learning, in instrumentalizing teacher education, lost a fundamental notion; language and learning are human sciences—they can be understood only by understanding the development of meanings in people and what they want to accomplish.

This means that we must research in serious and creative ways a coherent framework for the ways in which our students come to know. We must recognize that we *cannot* do inquiry nor achieve insight by lectures, test scores, competency based certification programmes nor even by computers—the new messiahs linking mind and cosmos together but still fragmenting human discourse and learning.

I am convinced we will never achieve a coherent philosophy and practice of teaching and learning until all teachers have had opportunity to work it out for themselves. This means that we cannot separate the integration of knowledge even in an integrated curriculum from the learner who is integrating. This means that we can no longer afford the silly practice of pens flourishing in mindless classroom practices of note-taking in direct proportion to students' nervous energy to get it down for the sole purpose of spewing back information, facts on a test—evidence of having mastered someone else's knowledge. Surely beneath the neural synapses there are some naturally embedded questions to ask. For example, what contribution can a discipline like educational psychology make to coherently informing the theory and the practice of a secondary or elementary teacher and influencing the lives of her students? In seeking answers to genuine rather than trick questions to which we already know the answers, this means admitting, in Polanyi's sense, the reality of the natural groupings of the human mind—wanting to know something and supporting the efforts of those willing to accept the challenge. We need more experience in the realm of making grounded judgments, more rummaging around in our data and the data of our lives to see the possible meanings and the effect on the lives of others. We know that to learn to drive an automobile, you don't need a lesson on the combustion engine; but, we don't know yet how to make our students, as Seymour Papert says in *Mindstorms*, "learn how to fall in love with gears," shape learning into something that is aesthetically, humanly and authentically pleasing.

I would like to end with a language story an English as a second language teacher recounted to me a few weeks ago. He returned to school late in the afternoon after a professional development workshop; one of his 5th graders saluted him with the greeting—"Where are you going?" This teacher, well practised in correcting ESL students' language and feeding back the correct form, said—"You mean where am I coming from," to which the child replied—"No, where are you going? I haven't a clue where you're coming from."

Where we are coming from is a problematic issue in our profession. What we are trying to become in this International Federation for the Teaching of English presents us with a challenge. The essence of teacher education, however, learning for that matter at all levels, is how to make people—teachers, students and researchers—aware of their own meanings and the meanings of others.

REFERENCES

Goodlad, J. I. (1984). *A Place Called School: Prospects for the Future*. New York, McGraw-Hill Co.
Hart, L. (1983). *Human Brain and Human Learning*. New York: Longman.
Polanyi, M. (1969) in *Knowing and Being* (M. Greene, Ed.) Chicago: University of Chicago Press.

Hidden Impediments

JAMES MOFFETT

Mariposa, California (U.S.A.)

For the last twenty years, I have sought to help reform the language arts curriculum.* During these twenty years, both applied research in teaching methods and basic research in verbal/cognitive processes have increased substantially. We now know much more than in 1964 about how people use language and how they might be helped to improve their use of it. But more classroom innovation was taking place in the '60s than is taking place now in the '80s. And most of the advances made in that progressive era have been erased by regressive trends that began in the mid '70s. If greater knowledge leads to better action, why are most schools going backwards, retrenching into materials and methods long since tried and found untrue? What are the obstacles that thwart the best efforts to improve discursive learning and that flout the knowledge accumulated by research?

I know, it *seems* that exciting change is breaking through all over. If you were to judge from what you might read in our professional journals, hear at our conferences, find in school districts' goal statements, and encounter in some preservice training or inservice workshops . . . well, you would think that the joint was jumping. (It may be, but more from institutional agitation than from curriculum innovation.) But if you leave this hubbub of bright shoptalk and go into the classroom itself—ignore what the adults are saying and look at what the kids are doing—you will find little of what you have heard about. It's as if the teacher and the language arts consultant must check their understanding at the classroom door.

Although I have conferred and consulted some in Canada and Australia, I would not presume to say how much the following remarks may apply to countries other than the U.S., where the experience underlying them was acquired.

Educators know far more about language learning than they enact, and many teachers are doing what they do not believe in, because they are not free. Resigned, or just glad to have a job, many usher their charges through an insultingly robotic reading program or grammar/composition textbook series that they despise and that even its own publisher scorns, all the while deftly plugging it into the tidy managerial systems and the back-to-basics mystique. Other teachers, wanting to believe in what they are told to do, try to rationalize; you don't think deeply about what you have no power over. When I recommend individualized reading and writing, small-group process, and a broader range of oral and written discourse, teachers commonly say, "I think you're right, but I can't do those things in my school."

Fired up by even a summer institute in the National Writing Project, the best curricular movement I know of, all too often the teacher ends sooner or later by putting all these exciting activities wistfully aside because certain required things have to be put before them—the competency tests taught to, the Warriner's books used— and somehow the occasions, the means, never materialize. True, a few remarkable educators have done what is mostly only talked about—got children writing and revising with the self-concept of professionals, or started up small-group discussion or the writing workshop—but too often they are operating in specially arranged situations, often experimental. When the person, the funds, the circumstances disappear, so does the activity, for nothing in the school organization or philosophy makes certain that it will continue.

Educators today commonly regard research as the key to curricular change, but what is holding up the improvement of the language arts curriculum isn't lack of knowledge. Those teachers who have been enfranchised as well as enlightened have always found how to teach reading and writing successfully long before research was attempting to show them how. We don't need a laboratory to see how people who read and write well become involved and adept. We don't need special studies to tell us that the language opportunities offered in school are almost invariably inferior to those of an optimal learning environment, or that if teachers shut up and let kids talk they would both learn more. We already know perfectly well that oral activities such as small-group discussion and improvisations will pay off for reading and writing.

John Mellon and I spent a good part of two years in the '60s trying to prove that cognitive development would result from small-group discussion, an impossible task because there is no one-to-one correspondence between thought and language that would enable improved thinking to show *scientifically* in transcripts. Then I realized we weren't trying to *discover* something that no one knew; we were convinced already, as anyone would be who had spent much time teaching or observing children or even noting his own discursive processes. What we were really trying to do was come up with scores that would embarrass schools into honoring and instituting serious oral-language activities. The experts we consulted in research quantification said, "Why sweat it? Just tell us what you want to prove and we'll show you how to make the figures come out right. It's all bull anyway." Actually, no amount of proof would have made effective oral-language activities a *staple* of the language arts curriculum even in the '60s. If it's not tested, it's not taught. There were other reasons than lack of evidence that prevented this sorely needed implementation. The matter partakes more of politics than of science.

The current focus and reliance on research distracts us from the true causes of ineffectual and irrelevant methods of teaching. Partly, this preoccupation with research is a kind of whistling in the dark to keep up our courage. Partly, it simply supports some educators and researchers who depend on it for funding, academic recognition, and job advancement. I say this actually with considerable sympathy. (Some of my best friends are researchers.) Educators based in a university may find that unless they scientize their work by casting it as experimental research, they may well be unable to stay on in an academic setting. This is especially true in the field of composition, which has seldom been regarded in universities as more than a menial trade having no body of content, like history or literature or physics, and thus can't be staffed, as the subject fields are, with tenure-track faculty. But at least, much research has shifted in recent years from statistical experimentation to case studies and ethnography, which are more congenial to the nature of composing. But we need not await the results of even this research to institute a fine writing curriculum, any more than we need hang suspensefully on the outcome of research comparing the efficacy of one school reading method with another when schools still don't practice the most efficacious methods enough for them to show on the scoreboard.

If lack of knowledge or evidence is not what blocks curriculum improvement, then what does? It's something that no one rushes pell-mell to examine—a set of mostly unconscious attitudes and emotions in both the public and the profession. Generally, the larger society places certain constraints and demands on schools that conflict with learning activities advocated by the most thoughtful educators. Most of the public wants schools to control the content of reading and writing, but so long as students don't gain experience finding and choosing content for themselves they remain essentially unengaged with school work, except to "get through" (if they don't actually drop out), and never learn to make for themselves the decisions that lie at the heart of composing and comprehending. Furthermore, both laity and educators fear the liberation in thought and behavior that students would achieve if talking, reading, and writing were taught most effectively; that is, if these powerful tools were freely given to youngsters for their personal investigation. Parents and teachers are unconsciously hedging and stalling on implementing a successful language curriculum.

Let me try to analyze this formidable obstacle. First, most parents still want schools to reinforce home training by inculcating their values, heritage, and modes of behavior. ("Inculcate," by the way, means etymologically to "grind in with the heel.") This creates, for one thing, a conflict with educators. Whereas most parents want their children to stay the way they made them, most teachers regard learning and growth as change. The public wants schools to prepare youngsters for jobs and roles such as it grew up among. It wants to perpetuate a world it understood, limited to a particular era and culture. This is of course the real meaning of "back to basics." Consequently, when the public asks schools to teach its children to learn to read and write, to think and create, it does not entirely mean it. At least, it doesn't mean it as educators might, who know that growth entails change and that you can't both indoctrinate students and teach them to think for themselves. Only by the latter, certainly, will they survive in the future, when tradition cannot possibly serve well.

Most laymen believe that reading and writing should be taught by informing students of something they don't know, that is as vessel-filling, and error-correcting. Let's just note in passing how well this fits the assumption in our profession that as research better informs us, we can solve our teaching problems, which result from mere lack of information. From the assumption of an information deficit it follows that learning to read and write need not disturb cultural values, which indeed one expects schools to reinforce. But in fact reading and writing are very dangerous—at least as likely to transform as to transmit culture—and everyone knows this, however subterraneanly. Literacy bypasses the local oral culture of family and ethos and may acquaint youngsters with ideas and ways of life their parents ignore or abhor. As a way of carrying one's thought beyond received ideas, writing too may change youngsters. "Composing," after all, means "putting together." Composing is *making* sense. An authentic author is not a plagiarizer or paraphraser but someone who puts things together for himself or herself. Reading and writing *are* dangerous and have always been so regarded, which is essentially why literacy was restricted until the printing press made control of manuscripts impossible. Ruling classes in the past have always tried to prevent their subjects from acquiring such powerful instruments. In today's democracy, the ruling class are the adults, who are also obliged, however, to pass on these instruments. And so we do but with half a heart. We think double-mindedly about reading and writing because our contrary motives put us in a double bind.

Parents who fear losing their children—and the majority do in some way—want the content of reading and writing to be controlled or to be made different. Teach my children to read, but I don't want them to read that or that or that. Teach my children to write, but they don't need to delve into this or this or this. Just teach them to read and write so they can get good jobs. Such an attitude, steering ambivalently between the necessity of literacy and the threat it poses, ultimately delivers to schools the message that they should teach youngsters to read just well enough to follow orders and to write just well enough to take dictation. The content of reading is controlled by limiting reading to textbooks, which adoption committees and publishers make certain don't contain anything that most parents don't want their children to think about. Efforts to censor books in public schools and libraries have increased at a shocking rate since the mid '70s. It is well known that many U.S. publishers put out only materials they believe to have potential for adoption in such lucrative states as Texas.

If parents and educators conflict somewhat on the issue of change in students, they also unwittingly conspire somewhat to control content. Many schools prefer a heavy emphasis on phonics for teaching literacy and an atomistically programmed treatment of reading comprehension because these are easier to administer and evaluate than an individualized reading program, which permits choice of subject matter, activates the intellect, and fosters a far greater quantity of reading. For years I marveled that laymen ordinarily unconcerned with pedagogy should take up the cudgels for the literacy method called phonics until I realized that they value it precisely because the drills with word particles or isolated words constitute the most meaningless approach, the one most devoid of content. (I don't say that *teachers* are necessarily attracted to phonics for this reason.) In other words, a contentless method seems an ideal way to render reading innocuous. A heavy phonics emphasis is preferred because it appears to teach reading while crippling it. The U.S. is full of kids—and adults—who passed the so-called reading tests but can't read, because those are really just *phonics* tests; who passed the comprehension quizzes with their snippets of indifferent content and plodded through all those disinfected textbooks controlled for everything from vocabulary and sentence complexity to topics and ideas but who won't read now unless they're flogged into it and who if they can in fact read will hide the fact from the authorities. They never saw reading as a personal resource with which to do what *they* want to do.

But what about books out of school? Won't *they* rob us of our children's minds and alientate their affections? Well, precisely, if you choose the right teaching methods, youngsters will never *want* to read outside and so will do it only when the next boss down the line forces them. People read for content, for what the text is about and can do for them. To the extent that the teaching methods and materials neutralize subject matter and mobilize anxiety they fail to engage the mind and the will. Then of course nothing works, and literacy falsely appears to be hard to learn, even when twelve years are squandered on it.

Don't get me wrong. I don't think parents and educators deliberately undermine reading and writing while extolling them and giving them priority as so-called basic skills. But all adult parties have reasons to fear reading and writing that we are not acknowledging. This causes us to deal with reading and writing in a double-minded way and hence to sabotage our own alleged goals. Laymen fear loss of control over the minds of the young, from which would seem to follow rejection of adult values and change in the social and moral order—revolution. But if adult society as a whole fears losing the minds of the young, teachers in particular fear losing their own minds if they try to teach the way they know they should. They fear loss of classroom control and of status if they allow youngsters to choose the content and form of what they read and write. Making the student active and the teacher reactive seems like a gratuitous relinquishing of power. But empowering is the teacher's job. Which of them, however, have been trained to decide how to teach decision-making, to liberate instead of restrict? Even those who do try are most often eventually stymied by requirements and edicts decided over *their* heads.

Two main alternative methods for teaching literacy and reading are the language-experience approach, whereby learners dictate what they have to say while looking on, and the read-along or lap method, whereby children follow on the page as someone reads to them something they want to hear and eventually be able to read for themselves.

Content is uncontrolled because the learner chooses what to say and hear. The aide merely acts as a temporary intermediary between learner and text until through massive experience in simultaneously seeing and hearing the language the learner takes over this role for himself or herself. In combination with plentiful small-group talk to develop the oral base, such methods foil completely the traditional classroom scenario casting the teacher as the star of the show and making of the pupils an audience, because these methods all call for decentralized classroom management permitting individuals to work together either in small parties with each other or with aides, while the teacher circulates among them all.

To focus now on writing, here too schools have a powerful reason to thwart all the best expert advice, research, and up-to-date understanding. Parents have not needed to crusade for censorship of writing because U.S. educators have not asked students to do much real writing and when they have, they usually supply students with the subject matter they want them to write about. The negative feeling acquired early toward writing from Prussian handwriting exercises plus the generally mechanistic literacy practices already referred to ensure that learners no more choose to write on their own than choose to read on their own. On the many occasions when I have asked teachers to recall learning to write, most have said the positive experiences occurred out of school and that school writing was associated with pain and failure.

Some lucky elementary children may be allowed to write on contents and in forms that they choose, but most are still licking their wounds from learning handwriting and spelling when they begin the first of the endless writings about a given content, about what they were told to read or simply just about what they were told. It begins with the paraphrasing of reference sources called "reports" and the plot summaries called "book reports," which are really just checks on the directed reading. It continues through the "critical papers," "research papers," "term papers," and "essay questions" of high school and college right on into the "review of the literature" section of the doctoral thesis. What all this writing has in common is that it monitors assigned reading and tests coverage of the given content. Inasmuch as the reading material is controlled, the content of the writing is automatically controlled also.

Only marginally do students do other kinds of writing in their whole academic career. Most universities don't give a fig for composition courses as anything other than a way of servicing the testing practices of their other courses. Consequently, rarely has writing been seriously honored and taught for its own sake in all its variety of forms and purposes, as a central humanistic mode of knowing, which is how it would attract youngsters. Instead, reading and writing are brought into a stupefying negative relationship to each other that makes students want to avoid both. Every time you read, you have to write something about the text to show you got the point. That is, the punishment for reading is having to write. Both are something that others want for their own purposes, not something I want for mine.

Writing to test can at least be real writing, some sort of essay, even if the content and purpose constrain it to a given topic and a very limited type of essaying. Worse is the conversion of writing into a downright fraudulent set of exercises called "composition" that isn't writing at all but in fact a kind of decomposition—some atomizing of the writing process into pieces that can be studied and tested like any other factual content. Isolated dummy sentences and paragraphs are analyzed, ticketed, combined, sequenced or edited. The College Board test called "composition" has made this fraud respectable and set a terrible example of what you can get away with by converting a squirmy verb into a placid noun, by thingifying action to suit cheap multiple-choice tests. Again, as with reading, writing becomes safely eviscerated and decorticated. (No, I won't say "emasculated," because writing is both male and female.) Not only is the content of writing preempted by assigned reading and required topics but even the act of writing itself is converted to content. Reading about writing, like writing about the reading, burlesques the ideal of integrated learning. Killing two birds with one stone is hardly desirable if you want the birds to thrive. So in writing too we educators have reinforced that part of the public psyche that secretly tries to sabotage the key learning activities that help people think for themselves.

The solution of this problem calls for a new covenant between school and home. Educators will have to take the initiative and enlist laity in the teaching of those very processes of inquiry they distrust. For one thing, becoming involved in school reading and writing may keep parents from feeling that they are losing their children. For another thing, literacy should be taught socially, through other people, like initial speech itself, as a kind of incorporation into the human community, not as isolated drills with materials and machines. Language-experience and read-along are best suited for this and would ensure that hearts and minds are engaged in reading and writing from the outset. To serve best, these methods do require pairing a learner with an aide who takes down the dictation and reads aloud until the learner can decode and encode for himself or herself. These aides can be any literate adults, including senior citizens, but older youngsters from other grades make fine aides too. Children must feel that literacy is a powerful gift that all elders are freely and gladly passing on to them.

Beyond literacy itself, truly successful teaching of reading and writing, speaking and thinking, requires drastic re-deployment of human resources that only far closer collaboration between laity and educators will bring about. The three keys to improving the curriculum are (1) individualization of the learning tasks so that individuals are frequently doing different things from one another at the same time; (2) interaction among individuals for oral language development and the benefits of small-group dynamics in all of the language arts; and (3) integration of learning across subjects, media, and kinds of discourse so that individuals may continuously synthesize their own thought structures. Developing a curriculum based on individualization, interaction, and integration depends on a far greater involvement of the lay community than is now the tradition—for several reasons. One is economic.

Schools are going broke, but economic crisis could be a good thing. Schools will *have* to utilize paraprofessionals, and teachers will *have* to welcome them. As the public refuses to increase school funds, on grounds that they just need to use more effectively what they already have, it will become apparent that, in lieu of money, many people will need to help out in schools in order to keep them going. Many underemployed workers or overeducated professionals may find great satisfaction in becoming free educational paraprofessionals. Such a shift of human resources would end once and for all the dominance of the emcee or nervous-hostess model of classroom organization and facilitate instead the individualization and interaction necessary for student independence.

Once the laity *overtly* plays a major role in schooling, then it will have to share accountability for results instead, as now, of holding teachers solely responsible for success or failure while not according them a decision-making power commensurate with this responsibility. Moreover, I feel sure that the public will in this way become disenchanted with our current testing practices. Perhaps these other adults will come to realize that what in school is called "reading" isn't real reading, that what is called "composition" isn't real writing, and that this fraud has arisen partly from the double-bind in which they have placed schools.

Then I think we may not only see an end of scapegoating schools for social ills but also a beginning of realism in teaching reading and writing, because as representatives of the public, paraprofessionals can break the double-bind while providing the greater human resources needed to make the alternative work. Literacy needs to be taught in the same organic social way that children learn to speak at home. Literature should be an endless extension of bedtime stories. The writing curriculum should reflect what adults write in all their various vocations and avocations and should recapitulate the processes that characterize writing outside of school.

Students who have mastered literacy and are exploring all the kinds of discourse and disciplines need access to people who practice these—scholars, government officers, crafts people, journalists, lawyers, scientists, case workers, merchants, and so on. By role-playing adults in various occupations, young people not only prepare realistically for joining the adult world but also become familiar with the whole range of utilitarian, literary, and scientific discourse. Whereas younger pupils learning literacy need outsiders to come in and help them, older students need to be able to sally forth from school to observe or do apprenticeship at other sites. The community should help students arrange experience that will allow them to investigate this world they are expected to join and take over. As it is now, schools worry about liability suits because they are held responsible for students during school hours. But that is precisely the sort of difficulty that can be worked out with the community. Both school and community have to be willing to let students find out what is going on in the world and not try to control the content of what they will perceive, discuss, reflect on, and read and write about.

The worst of our joint hypocrisy has been to worship critical thinking, on the one hand, even to the point of biasing the whole national curriculum toward the climactic production of so-called critical essays as tests in university courses, while never inviting students to cut their intellectual teeth on their own environment. We cannot do all the selecting of subjects and topics and frameworks that students are to think about and within and still honestly expect them to become independent critical thinkers. Quality education requires that students circulate freely through that society they will one day run and critique it under the auspices of those currently running it.

Economic hard times may result in another boon—dropping textbooks. Aside from the fact that many textbook programs are political footballs by virtue of—I should say "by vice of"—requiring the approval and the financial commitment of some government, textbooks often pervert the teaching of the language arts in particular by the very fact of working against individualization and interaction and against the integration of the language arts with each other and these in turn with the other media and subject areas. Basal readers, literature series, and so-called composition or rhetoric textbooks merely get in the way by overcontrolling the reading matter—slowing, doling, and stereotyping—and by converting writing into just one more thing to study *about* instead of *do.*

In addition to what students write themselves, which in a good program would be considerable, the community can easily supply more and better reading material than textbooks have ever offered. Teachers, specialists, laymen, and librarians can help students to organize all these contributions physically, for access, and mentally for individual reading programs. Of course straight anthologies of literature have often been compiled for schools, but even anthologies are often thematically organized or include other material to direct thinking. Though certain compendiums of information created for young people may be justified in empirical subjects such as the social and natural sciences, the language arts are not empirical subjects but rather, precisely, *arts*, activities, practices, not themselves fit objects for required study by youngsters. For these reasons I have never myself consented to create school books other than anthologies of readings.

It is extremely dangerous to buy curricula, especially as these are packaged by large corporations, which in today's world are essentially amoral. Just as state and local school boards implement the public's hidden fear of learning, publishers enshrine these fears in materials that become in turn imposing models of schooling and influence the public's notion of learning, because everyone passes through them as children.

In combination with economic crisis, the increasing pluralism of communities also makes imperative some new covenant between school and home. Just as financial hard times could actually improve education, so could the staggering diversity of ethnic, linguistic, national and religious groups with which the traditional open-door policies of Anglo-Saxon countries have flooded their schools. No longer will it be possible to pretend to educate well by a single, standardized curriculum. A pluralistic society must have a pluralistic curriculum, which is to say that the individualization that should long ago have determined the main organization of schooling may now be forced upon us. Learners are different and need different things. Their parents differ about what they think schools should do for them. Individuals differ by both personal make-up and ethnic background. Voucher systems would prove more, not less, expensive and would institute rather than solve conflict and social fragmentation. If you're all broke but differ, and have to share the same resources, you have an opportunity for an extraordinary education enterprise. Everyone will have to cooperate to get what each one's differences require. In accommodating group differences out of necessity, schools will finally be able to allow also for individual differences, because once we abandon the insistence on standardization, we will see how to organize resources for learners to be doing different things at the same time throughout a community that has become a large school. A major reason for standardizing has been to facilitate evaluation so that educators would be accountable to laymen. But the more that hard times force laymen to participate in schooling, and the more that this pluralistic public gives schools conflicting ultimatums, the more the fiction must break down that educators alone determine how they are to proceed and are therefore solely accountable for learning results.

Instead of pretending that as research returns come in we will improve our teaching, let's begin to acknowledge that we will improve our teaching when we stop colluding unconsciously with the public to thwart our own fearsome goal of teaching youngsters to think for themselves and, instead, initiate with the public a deliberate and full collaboration. Neither of us needs fear loss of power and identity. Things are out of control now. And one reason kids are so hard to handle is that they feel that we are not doing what we profess but are in fact using school as a holding tank to prevent them from exploring a world they never made but are going to have to live in. This makes them build up enormous resentment and suspect that adults are fraudulent and hypocritical. Then indeed we do lose their minds. We must give them reading and writing as *theirs*, as human rights, and not give them with one hand and take them back with the other.

Broaching this problem with the public means laying out to them something such as what I have tried to say here, though probably with more tact, which is not so necessary in shoptalk with colleagues. Most educators have a good idea of how learning stands to be improved and deeply long to make significant changes. Inasmuch, however, as the obstacles involve our relationship with the society that commissions us to teach its youth, it is with that society that we have to work out solutions.

English Teaching:
Art and Science

GARTH BOOMER
Curriculum Development Centre,
Canberra (Australia)

Part One: The Curriculum Text

Mrs. Bell, a teacher of ten years' experience in the one school, has begun a unit of work at Timbertown High School in Australia with her year 10 (15-year-olds) English class of twenty-one. The school is in a predominantly working class area but is essentially an academic institution. The setting is a second floor semi-enclosed classroom in a former open space section of the school built to accommodate eight such classrooms. Noise drifts in around partitions and through concertina dividers from classes next door. We cannot take in everything and everyone and so we concentrate on Tammy, a vivacious Greek-Australian, Guiseppe, known as Joseph, of Italian descent, the inifinitely self-effacing Au Kim, newly arrived from Vietnam, and Brenton, the ocker Australian who carries a cricket bat with him everywhere like a wand to ward off evil, occasionally using it as a mock machine gun on his enemies. Progressively over a two-month period we will get to know each member of the class, as, like a negative becoming positive in developing fluid, they emerge and are particularized in our awareness. They have been with the teacher for only five weeks. They are to read the Ruth Park novel, *Playing Beatie Bow*, the story of a present-day Sydney girl Abigail, who is taken back one hundred years in time to live with her ancestors. The experience helps her to understand her confused adolescence and to come to terms with her parents' separation.

Early in the unit of work we find Mrs. Bell reading the third chapter, pausing to show pictures from a book on colonial Sydney.

This address was delivered at the 74th annual meeting of the National Council of Teachers of English in Detroit immediately following the IFTE Seminar. Garth Boomer is former Chair of IFTE.

101

After some reading she stops to negotiate with the class about how the rest of the book is to be read. Tammy suggests they read in groups, not friendship groups but groups that will be "best for you." Homework is to find quotations in the early chapters which relate to Abigail's "inner conflict."

The next lesson is two days on. The entry to the class is ragged and noisy. Mrs. Bell pauses patiently for attention. Joseph is not eager to begin. When Mrs. Bell announces that she is pregnant, Brenton raises a laugh by asking "How far gone?" They all edge forward to clarify the details of when she will be leaving. Mrs. Bell lets them know exactly when she will take leave (five months hence).

Groups are given contract sheets to fill in, indicating to the teacher how they intend to carry out the reading assignment and what time line they will use. Brenton repeatedly seeks teacher attention as Mrs. Bell circulates answering questions of clarification about the contract and the task. Eventually they begin to read, some silently, some in groups. Brenton can be overheard telling Joseph about "midwives": "In olden days they had grannies who helped people have kids." Au Kim and Lai Anh read alone with immense concentration, and Tammy chatters volubly postponing the task.

Later in the lesson, as requested by Mrs. Bell, they negotiate themselves into new friendship or "convenience" groups and each group receives a worksheet which asks them to establish what is meant by "self-awareness," "inner conflict," and "in search of inner self" in relation to the novel. It is suggested that they brainstorm personal examples and then report to the class. After this they are each to prepare a reading/performance or presentation of a poem which reveals one of these themes, explaining how it relates to the novel. The instruction reads:

Decide how the group will go about this.
In what way can the group support each other?
How will you present the poems and your reactions?
Decide on group and individual tasks.

Brenton wants to work individually, but seeing all the others in groups, he approaches two very conscientious workers, Cain and Phillip, who quite patently do not want him. Reluctantly, however, they grant him entry.

Mrs. Bell is busy explaining "inner conflict," clarifying time lines and answering "commissions" from students, especially from the irrepressible Brenton who sends out frequent mock radio messages: "Calling Mrs. Bell, calling Mrs. Bell . . . ."

Eavesdropping on Joseph's group, we discover them talking about shoplifting and smoking, while from another group of girls we overhear: "Sodium's *Na.*" The previous lesson in science has carried over. Glen companionably wanders across to tell Tammy's group to be quiet and stays to yarn. Joseph yawns, takes out his watch, shakes it and announces that it has had a cardiac arrest. When it comes to silent or group reading time, Brenton paces the room like a caged tiger asserting that he has finished. Mrs. Bell, with great patience, suggests a range of extension novels which she has brought along for this very purpose, and causing our eyebrows to lift slightly, Brenton eventually settles down ostentatiously with *Dr. Zhivago.* After six pages he re-enters a group and announces that Abigail is a "schizophrenic antidisestablishmentarian."

We note, by the way, that each lesson begins with very explicit recapitulation by Mrs. Bell about what has happened, along with reminders about where the work is heading and how it is to be organized. After the weekend, the teacher brings in a good range of poetry anthologies and talks with the whole class about how to use the library to find more poetry. Before long, after leafing through the anthologies, most of them containing poems by children of about their own age, they begin to read pieces to each other. "Listen to this one," "I've found one."

Joseph's group discusses cricket until Glen interrupts. He has found a poem about a drag race between rival gangs. Joseph laughs. Glen suggests a group poem about "The Street Machine" and they begin tossing in lines. The effort falters; Chris announces that he's going to write about "The Lifestyle of a Rice Bubble," while Michael and Glen take out a motor magazine and look at the pictures. Eventually, they pause to hear Chris's poem. Mrs. Bell approaches and they all give the impression of serious work. Without destroying the rice bubble initiative, she reminds them of the need to find poems about inner conflict. She directs them back to the task sheet. She suggests that they might find a whole range of ways to present their work dramatically.

A couple of lessons on, Mrs. Bell takes two groups who seem to be making little headway and suggests that she provide a model of how to analyse a poem and find aspects of its themes. "What do you think?" she asks and, with little enthusiasm it seems, they agree. She reads the poem "At Sixteen" and they jot down "what the poem is about" except for Joseph who can't find his paper. While other groups argue and negotiate about how to perform their poems, Mrs. Bell is still at work on her modelling exercise. Now she is at the point of reading them her own piece on "At Sixteen" showing them how she interweaves quotation and commentary.

At another table Brenton and his two conscientious colleagues are preparing a poster, the centre of which is a huge brain around which they attach poems on inner conflict. Brenton announces that this was his idea. The other two repudiate the claim.

A joint decision that their work will be videotaped galvanizes formerly tardy groups. It takes three more lessons to complete the performances, which contain some real surprises. Brenton, for instance, performs passionately and well the role of a drug addict and wins acclaim from those who usually find him a pain. The camera is forgotten. The Vietnamese girls, still shy, get through their parts, while Joseph and Glen take the acting award with a fine piece on racial discrimination. Each performance is followed by constructive evaluation from Mrs. Bell and the class.

Two events serve as the end points. In one lesson the whole class reflects on what they have learnt and a couple of weeks later sit rapt and fascinated watching the video replay of their achievements.

Part Two: A Student Perspective

Throughout the enactment of this particular English curriculum text, we have had the privilege of talking at the end of each lesson to Tammy, Au Kim, and Joseph about what happened, what they thought of what happened, and what they thought might happen next. In the early interviews with the students we note an almost total lack of empathy with the teacher as teacher. They do not perceive that what she is doing is premeditated and constantly reworked in the light of their response to her planning. When asked to predict what Mrs. Bell will do next they are at first working simply on their general knowledge of "what English teachers do." "She's getting us to underline things, so probably at the end she'll get us to write that up and then write an essay on it," says Tammy.

While they begin with a very poor understanding of why they are doing what they are doing, despite Mrs. Bell's persistent and patient reiteration at the beginning of each lesson and during lessons, they are aware that English this year is different: "We are going deeper into things this year," says Joseph.

Some way into the unit such self-consciousness emerges in the interviews. Tammy, reflecting upon a group work session, shows a grasp of some things we might wish more teachers to appreciate: "It was good. If we didn't understand, we'd share it around the group. When we got really stuck, we called her over and figured it out. Once you're in groups, you don't feel scared about whether it's right or wrong, you can just say it." Not all of them perceive that they have *worked:* "We didn't do too much work. Writing work. It was all reading and getting into groups. Talking. We didn't get much work done." Clearly work is acquainted with writing.

While they are inarticulate about Mrs. Bell's and their own intentions early in the unit, towards the end they are highly articulate, expansive and detailed in their prediction about what is going to happen. Indeed their remarks take on very similar qualities to the monologue planning texts of Mrs. Bell herself. They become, over time, co-planners of the curriculum.

"Tuesday we're probably going to go back into our reading groups—a lesson of that. Wednesday we don't have English. Thursday we've got a double lesson, so I think one lesson we're going to be performing it and it will probably run into the next lesson and then Friday—the next two lessons we'll probably rehearse—and perform it again. And the week after that, earlier than expected, we'll probably show the play."

They also show themselves to be aware of each other in more than superficial ways: "How do you explain Brenton?" the interviewer says. "He wants attention," says Tammy. "Mm," says Joseph. "He's got problems," says Tammy. "You know, home and all that. Personal problems. Doesn't get enough love and attention at home."

They do much better empathizing with Brenton than they do with Mrs. Bell. Despite her openness about herself and her own experience in class discussions, an occlusion operates. She is a teacher: "I don't think teachers worry about many things," says Tammy.

They find it almost impossible to talk about what she might have felt or thought about a lesson: "But don't you try to read your teacher's mind?" says the interviewer. "Only when there's a test coming up," says Joseph.

When it is all over they interestingly contradict themselves. They have not worked and yet they say they have learnt "bulk about poems," gained confidence which will help them get a job, survived the test of performing to their peers ("It will be much easier next time") and furthermore they understand that they have been allowed to work through some of the darker areas of adolescence.

"It helps you to get feelings out of your head."

Part Three: Inside the Teacher's Mind

We have seen the unfolding drama. We have heard the spectator/participant comments of some students. Now we are allowed the unique experience of eavesdropping on the mind of the teacher in her initial composing, during the enactment of the curriculum unit and in reflection on the work done. She has tried to capture the life of her mind by speaking a running commentary monologue of her thoughts into a hand-held tape recorder. In the essentially privatized world of education, educational writers have been prone to stigmatize and stereotype teachers, reducing them to types and styles; speculating, often patronizingly, about intentions and designs. But we are to come close to a direct window on the mind of the practitioner at work. We who have been teachers, too, recognize it as authentic. This archaeological exercise reminds us of treasures we tend to bury and forget; things we know but do not speak of when we write about the art and science of our own teaching; perhaps so taken for granted that we de-value them.

In the incubating stages Mrs. Bell loosely construes the unit. Her preference is to use the novel *The Outsiders* by Ruth Park because "it works well with year 10s." She wants to set up group collaboration on writing and she is keen to introduce extension reading. She is not happy yet with their contribution to class discussion. She hopes that in groups she can structure things so that they feel comfortable to exchange ideas.

Following the flow sometime later, we are reminded that schools are complex contexts: "Well, *The Outsiders* is not available. In fact, I'm sixth on the list in application for it. Its popularity is spreading alike with teachers and students. *Romeo and Juliet* looks as though it couldn't be arranged in time, so *Playing Beatie Bow* it is."

She begins to spark ideas off herself: "I'd like some to take a literary criticism type approach . . . I think some get enjoyment out of using their skills as writers, their skills of honing down their thoughts. I can certainly remember at year 10 level myself starting to feel that come together in the pure enjoyment of it. . . . But it also lends itself really well to an exploration of the historical aspects of the novel and the idea of time travel which is an element of this story, and I think we could look into that particularly because of its Australian setting, although it wouldn't have to be confined to Australia. . . ."

From this consideration she moves on to think about stream of consciousness writing in journals and this leads her to the idea which from our vantage point we know finally takes the central ground: "I think poetry is another area. I think I'd do that before we get into writing at the end of the novel. Poetry that takes up one of the themes of the book, of growing personal awareness of the inner conflict that the girl is going through . . . It's an area that year 10s are into themselves. . . . Last year we started a poem called *At Sixteen* and there was lots of response to that poem . . . and then I invited them to find poems that they thought expressed conflict. . . . I also suggested that they might like to write poems. . . . That was really good . . . So I would really like to capture some of that again this year. The poetry would be something that we would do. Yes . . . that is something I will do for sure."

Then she plunges deep into the content of the novel exploring its themes and symbols, testing the limits of its territory and its relevance to the students. She dwells for some time on the problems of the Vietnamese students who will need extra help. We leave her first monologue at the point where she will now write up the curriculum unit, along with some structures for them to work within . . . "a framework for them to choose their own sorts of work and set their own questions. . . ."

As the work begins we listen to her contemplating some of the surprise turns in the plot: "There was a group who opted to read with me who were not weak students who might be looking for help and guidance. In fact, those chose not to work with me. Those who did are quite confident readers who said they enjoyed discussing their reading and reflecting on the novel as they went along. . . ."

She is critical of her ambiguous or unclear wording on the task sheets and acknowledges the confusion, "although they came up with some good ideas in groups." Within the commentary on the content and process of the lessons are embedded observations on the students: "Brenton went and sat himself with Cain and Phillip much to their displeasure but he stood his ground."

"Kim and Anh showed their usual reluctance to join a group. I don't know whether it's because they don't want to join a group or because of their shyness; they think perhaps they're not welcome. And I suggested to them that Tammy and Elvira's group would make them welcome having asked them if it was OK with them. They're very friendly and Kim and Anh came over quietly. But I was impressed by the way the other girls made them welcome and they seemed to settle in quite well there. . . ."

Since Brenton has already forced us to attend to him, it is worth following what Mrs. Bell thinks about him: "I put some pressure on him early in the piece of work, an unfinished piece . . . and his comment to me was: 'Oh, what are you bothering for; nobody else does'. . . . I think Brenton interrupts and does his usual thing with the cricket bat . . . to make his presence felt. That's his way of making contact. It doesn't particularly worry me."

Quite extensively she expands upon her theories of teaching the novel, particularly dwelling on the perspectives she brings as an historian. She also reflects upon the quality of student work: "There's still not as much commitment to the work as I'd hoped . . . especially from being able to work in groups. I feel it's been a bit slow this week. There's always that time factor. There's so much we could do in relation to the novel . . . but I feel a bit restricted by time. This week I hope that the interest in the poetry will really get going."

A week later she is more satisfied: "The week finished on quite a high note. . . . People seemed to be really getting into the poetry. Tammy's group has quite an exciting notion of threading their poems into a play. However, a couple of groups seem a bit baffled by the open-ended nature of the task."

In explaining her decision to take two groups aside for some intensive "modelling," she enters into some detailed theorizing: "I'll be trying to show them by example, by getting them to do things I would do in coming to grips with the poem. . . . Obviously I'd already chosen it because I feel that it is suitable . . . but later we can go back with a better awareness to their choices. . . . So I'm trying to show them how I would work, create a structure that they can take back and apply . . . and also show them a bit of the excitement of coming to terms with a poem they at first may not have a positive re-action to . . . the excitement of working through until you feel you've come to grips with the poem . . . and I'll actually write with them."

Her relief and pleasure show as she comments on what eventually happens: "Cain and Brenton and Phillip did their performance today. I think the class was half embarrassed . . . about Brenton's approach to his work, his passionate delivery. They were obviously interested in achieving a level of finished product that Brenton usually would not pay attention to.

Diane's confidence in front of the camera was amazing. I heard Linda say "How could she do it?" and I must admit I share Linda's awe . . . but it was a marvellous impassioned reading.

Joseph's little cameo role theme of the beer-drinking man watching TV I thought was excellent and yet despite all this he doesn't want to work in English. . . . But the group made him commit himself to the task and it was a real high point."

Looking back on the transcript of her incubation, she expresses satisfaction that, while the specifics changed, she achieved some of her broad intentions. With evident pleasure she recounts to herself what the class achieved, without overlooking the shortcomings: "They worked well together, they worked effectively, they worked perceptively."

Part Four: The Science and the Art

In thinking about how I should present to you my ideas about the science and art of English teaching, indeed all teaching, I have had many false starts. I knew I must ground my remarks. My privileged association with Mrs. Bell gave me such grounding to the point where it hurts. Again and again I have come back to my data, layer upon layer of complex insights into Mrs. Bell and her work. The more I have looked, the more awestruck I have become at the immensity of her achievement and the more angry I have become at myself and many other well-intentioned English educators who in the past have stood up at conferences and confidently sailed into learned analyses about English teachers and English teaching with varying degrees of meta-immunity from the territory. So often I have cleverly drawn maps without experiencing the terrain. This time, I knew, I must use this forum to celebrate the essentially unmappable, ineffable composing and acting of a fine teacher. This time, I must assail the teacher reducers and teacher bashers (often sadly you teachers yourselves), with a demonstration that would illustrate the relative bankruptcy of any one academic discipline in terms of the common wealth of teachers.

Mrs. Bell is a daVinci and a Galileo. In order to practise her craft at Timbertown High School in 1984, she needs a brilliant generic promiscuity. She must mix psychology, history, literature, politics, sociology, linguistics, economics, art, science, philosophy, poetics and aesthetics with passion and dispassion, with pragmatism and vision.

Aware that I had collected riches and treasures about English teaching that I had never found before, I knew nevertheless how inadequate my portrayal of Mrs. Bell to you would still be.

Mrs. Bell told me how inadequate her spoken monologues were in capturing what she really did when she composed. Even as we spoke about her teaching, she kept catching herself out in half-truths or inadequate representations of what she did and how she did it. She tended to depict herself as not having a learning theory and yet, as she talked, she realized, perhaps for the first time, the degree to which she deliberately and systematically operates on a coherent theory of teaching: "In retrospect, I realize that I've read many things that must have influenced me and I have actually written down my views about learning. When I teach I'm not conscious of these things, but as we sit here and talk, I realize that it is all there as a kind of fuel to my teaching."

So now, with the proviso that Mrs. Bell herself doubts her own veracity as a storyteller, that I captured only a fraction of the interaction in my lesson notes, that truth is always tangential, I will try in this part of my address to analyse some of what Mrs. Bell does, and in so doing I hope that, through one example, I might celebrate the Universal English Teacher. The picture I paint is one of infinite embeddedness. The teaching moment is set within the teaching sequence, set within a particular classroom of a particular school in a particular socio-political context at a particular moment of history. The participants can cause infinite variations from moment to moment, each coming from a distinct and complex setting, and each interpreting the moment differently.

I have sought appropriate analogies to capture what Mrs. Bell does. I considered the circus performer keeping a range of plates spinning on a pole. Then I thought of the script writer turned drama director. Finally, I concluded that teaching is like nothing else.

Taking Mrs. Bell's teaching apart is akin to dissecting a poem, but let me see if in order to sharpen our appreciation I can analyze just ten aspects of her repertoire, and then put her back together again.

She is:

1. *Indweller/Imaginer/Psychologist*

Mrs. Bell illustrates that one cannot teach without imagining, and imagining means being able to see events unfolding in contexts as well as being able to create a version of what it might be like in someone else's mind, particularly in the minds of learners.

The transcripts show the complex construing that goes on when a teacher incubates on a possible unit of work. Mrs. Bell conjures up last year's class and holds it alongside this year's class, balancing similarities and differences. She imagines what is possible with this group, this year, fielding in her mind how the whole class might respond while keeping a delicate hold on how different individuals might respond to the chosen novel.

She has to become a Vietnamese refugee, an unloved adolescent boy, a teenager in 1984, a poor reader and a high flier. As a base for these imaginings it seems that she needs first to become again herself at fifteen. This is her touchstone: "How did I feel about these things when I was their age?"

In order to teach Brenton and Au Kim she must progressively feel with them their confusion and their pleasures. She needs to build in herself an image of their present understandings in order to know when and how to teach them. She knows that only in those parts where she shares their dreams can she profitably teach.

2. *Experimenter/Theoretician/Scientist*

So alienating has been Mrs. Bell's undergraduate experience with *theory* that, like many of her colleagues, she does not consider herself a theoretician. *Theory* tends to be for those who theorize but don't teach. Yet the transcripts reveal a tenaciously theorizing mind at work operating deliberately and concertedly on established principles and procedures. Teaching may be an inexact science but it is nonetheless a science, in the sense that it cannot operate without the setting up of predictions about likely consequences in certain contexts. Just because there are multiple variables does not deny the need for science, the systematic pressing of present knowledge into new territory.

Let me list some of the principles and assumptions which help form Mrs. Bell's science: As Mrs. Bell says, these things are so "naturalized" for her that she is most of the time not conscious that they form part of her composing and enactment "generating plant."

a. *Collaboration:*
She knows that being in the company of others who are thinking aloud about how to do things and interacting with those people is a way to cognitive gain both about the "stuff" being explored and about how other people think and learn.

b. *Modelling/Demonstration:*
She knows that demonstration at the point of confusion is potent, if the learner really wants to overcome confusion.

c. *Extended Responses:*
Transcripts reveal that independent of Roger Brown, Ruth Weir and many other experts on language acquisition, Mrs. Bell learnt from her experience as a mother with her first child the subtleties of the complex linguistic dance which goes on between the learning child and adults. She realized for herself the power of the extended response which gives learners rich data upon which to base new forays into the world through language. Having deeply internalized this understanding, she operates on this with great patience, skill and empathy with her fifteen-year-old students.

d. *Performance and Production:*
She knows that skills are learnt and consolidated through application in tasks which have consequences. She also knows that the intention to perform or produce unlocks "tacit" powers (to use Polanyi's term).

e. *Answering Questions:*
Just as demonstration is important, so is question answering at the point of confusion. Mrs. Bell deliberately experiments in

this sequence of work with allowing students to experience confusion and to make mistakes. This is the mark of a confident and established theoretician. She knows that this will lead to her being commissioned to teach: "I set out to be even bolder in letting the kids take the wrong direction. I stood back more and let the questions come. . . ."

f. *Transformation:*

Mrs. Bell has not read Jerome Bruner on the theory of transformation (that each time we transform present understandings from one medium to another we increase our present understandings) and yet she knows the theory. The students read the novel. They then talk about the novel, through the medium of poetry. They then transform what they know into drama and into illustrations and posters. They write scripts and they read scripts. The series of transformations intensifies the learning. Mrs. Bell is quite deliberate in her planning for this to occur.

g. *Intention/Negotiation:*

Mrs. Bell has evolved over many years a very clear stance on the power of student intention as opposed to teacher coercion. She admits that she could have forced the class to be more superficially efficient in getting through the work. She could also have imposed a tighter, less negotiable structure. Instead she provided firm parameters within which she negotiated groupings, task allocations, and the form and content of assignments. She kept throwing the responsibility of choice and time management back onto the class. The result was a sequence where the class was slow to begin and floundering for a week or so. Gradually, as intentions and ownership took hold, the momentum gathered until in many ways the class took over. Her theories about withholding are linked with her strategies for empowerment. She has a very subtle understanding of the de-powering effects of premature instruction and direction.

An examination of Mrs. Bell's composing shows that in this sequence she also deliberately thinks aloud for students (linked with her theory of empowerment), that she insists on student self-evaluation for the same reason, and that she consistently requires prediction both about the outcomes of the novel and about the emerging shape of the unit of work.

As a scientist/teacher she is experimenting on a number of fronts in this sequence of work. Perhaps the most interesting exploration is her attempt to give them insight into her curriculum construction and to teach them how to construct their own curriculum.

The sub-text of this curriculum story deals with what it is to be a teacher and a learner. As an experimenter, Mrs. Bell is constantly construing and reconstruing in the light of her observation about what happens.

3. *Technician/Designer*
In her pre-teaching monologues, Mrs. Bell is somewhat like a painter before a blank canvas, looking at what she wishes to paint; using figurative hands to frame it in various ways in her mind and contemplating how to place it on the canvas. But this is a too static depiction of what she does. *Her* canvas is one which, she knows, will continually re-cast itself of its own volition. In designing her unit, she knows that she must take into account the counter-designs of the students. There is artistry in her imagining but the excitement of the vision is shaped and constrained by a wide range of technical and practical considerations.

Mrs. Bell has to take into account the nature of the classrooms, the availability of resources and materials, the time available (including the intervention of Sports Day and Easter), the school's assessment and reporting requirements and the present capabilities of the class. She has to consider questions of sequence, balance, and pace.

Implicit in any art or science is technology and skill in the manipulation of media. Mrs. Bell deploys oral, written, dramatic and visual media in a subtle blend to give colour, variety and changing tensions to her creation.

4. *Knower/Believer*
What does Mrs. Bell know in order to practise her art and science in this sequence of work? An adequate shopping list will give some idea. She knows about:

- Australian literature, Ruth Park as a novelist, and about this novel in particular;
- Australian history as it affects this novel;
- a range of poetry dealing with adolescent emotions similar to those in the novel;
- the various levels of work that might be expected of her 15-year-old students;
- the eventual requirements of examiners in English in terms of what constitutes a good literary/critical essay;
- the kind of diet that the class has had in the past and will have in the future; and
- the rationale of process writing.

To such knowledge, combined with her theories, she brings strong beliefs, the product of her particular socialization. She believes that:

- her job is to extend horizons so that students can move beyond their present world view;
- teachers should "come clean" on as many levels as possible;
- students' questions should be treated seriously;
- schools generally are repressive, secretive and confining;
- self-esteem is the cornerstone of learning;
- too many English teachers don't teach that which they hope students will learn; and
- that society should be based on sharing and collaboration.

Both art and science advance through theory from a base of knowledge under the direction of beliefs.

5. Controller/Shaper/Sculptor

Let's not be romantic. Mrs. Bell is in control. She has to be. What we haven't observed closely is the superb peripheral vision that allows her to move around the classroom settling pockets of unrest, unsettling ghettoes of idleness and provoking those who are sitting on their assets. There is a weaponry of gentle inquiry and reminder which she brings to this task. Most of the time she is one step ahead. She knows that Joseph, Glen and Michael are talking motor-bikes rather than inner conflict. They think they are getting away with it. She knows that there is value in the talk and allows it to develop a productive head of steam. She then delicately intervenes to re-direct the energy towards the formal task.

One way to look at what happens is to see it as a kind of physics of the classroom in which the law of conservation of energy operates, except that classrooms leak. Without vigilance, entropy will occur; the class resolve will wind down. Mrs. Bell is an anti-entropic agent redirecting and focussing energy. She also feeds energy by contributing her knowledge and ideas.

I had also thought to use the analogy of teacher as sculptor but clearly this is to deny the co-sculpting of students. In fact, we see Mrs. Bell early in the piece sculpting while the students are reluctant helpers or voyeurs. Then gradually the students take the basic clay shape and push it in directions unforeseen. At the end Mrs. Bell is admiring *their work.*

6. Coach/Demonstrator/Teacher

Mrs. Bell works with great commitment on an apprenticeship model. She deplores the way in which some of her colleagues expect students to pick up competencies by themselves. (The kind of teacher who puts encouraging or discouraging remarks on essays but never shows how to write an essay.)

She believes that it is her job to teach, to show, to explain. The students recognize and appreciate this. They know that they are going deep and that Mrs. Bell will help them when they are lost.

Mrs. Bell's talent lies in that subtle apprehension of when to tell and when to remain silent. She gets her cues from the students. When they genuinely ask, she teaches her heart out. If they don't ask and she feels strongly that they need her teaching and don't know it, she will impose herself, but only if she judges that the students are confused and will therefore pay attention to her demonstration. She must be assured that retrospectively they will appreciate what she has done.

In this sequence of work, she takes aside a small group to instruct them on how to read a poem, extract its themes and relate these to the novel. She does this by giving a very generous window on herself at work. She thinks for them, writes for them and comments in detail on why and how she does it. She is a coach who can do it. She is an empress who wears clothes!

7. *Metaphysicist/Illuminator/Commentator*

Mrs. Bell knows and shares my own interest in experimenting with teaching students to become theorizers about the teaching of their teachers and about their own learning. The slogan I use is "making the information and the theory available to the students."

If teachers are *deliberate* teachers, consciously operating on principles and clearly aware of why they use certain strategies to serve their intentions, *then* they can, if they wish, tell all of this to their students and invite them to see if it works. In this way, teachers can enlist the aid of students as laboratory assistants in the ongoing experiment. We observe Mrs. Bell explaining repetitiously why she is doing certain things, how she sees it working and what she thinks will be the benefits to them.

My recording of the students' comments show that early in the sequence they simply don't listen to this. Her explanatory spiels are treated almost like the opening credits for a film. Or perhaps more accurately, because schools generally don't require students to know why they are doing what they do, the explanations and the philosophizing go unregarded as a kind of noise or insignificant foreplay.

Significantly, later in the sequence the teacher's persistence is paying off. Students can not only indicate in detail what is happening and why, the also have clear goals that they are deliberately trying to reach. They can also comment on the learning advantages and disadvantages of group work and performance.

I am reminded of the story of the interns who met each week with specialists to examine x-ray prints. At first the bewildered interns watched without comprehension as the specialists discussed shadows the learners could not see. Eventually, they came to see what the specialists saw.

8. Politician/Battler

Behind the scenes of this teaching set, the politics of the school and the education system are fought out. Mrs. Bell in many ways teaches against the grain of the school and, sadly, of the English faculty itself. Allowing group work and a degree of student decision making is considered at least a mild form of insanity. Noise is the first sign of the dreaded disease "lack of control." People whisper pityingly behind hands about the unfortunates who can't keep their classes quiet.

Mrs. Bell has had painful crises of nerve when all the overt and covert signals of the school have said "Go back, you're going the wrong way." But, armed with her theory and her implacable desire to be congruent with her beliefs, she has persevered. Her greatest allies are her students and the parents of her students who know her commitment, her dedication and her record of *delivering* what she promises.

Her main protection is her articulate theory of education. With faculty heads, the school principal or outside questioners, she is strong in knowing why she teaches as she does. Opposition tends to wilt if it argues from dogma and entrenchment rather from rationality and understanding. Mrs. Bell has won room to move but it has taken her ten years. Recently she has become better at recruiting allies on the staff.

9. Provider/Servant

We have already discussed Mrs. Bell as formal demonstrator and question answerer. Her role as giver goes deeper than the more overt manifestations.

Between lessons she searches for books on early Sydney, finds and provides additional poetry anthologies, puts students in touch with extension novels and writes copious responses on written offerings. This is a servant role, largely unappreciated by the students. If students are to get on with the work, teachers must re-cast their role. For instance, because time was short at the end of the sequence, Mrs. Bell sensibly became an executive officer for the class committee: "We heard from each group, quickly, and then I undertook the task to write that up into a summary, which I will photocopy and give back to them."

10. *Connoisseur/Reflector/Critic*

Mrs. Bell's pre-teaching monologue, the reflections during the sequence and her retrospective comments, show clearly the role of the English teacher as savourer and mixer. This is the teacher as gourmet, checking for the right mix, testing effect and affect, worrying about unpalatable diversions and taking pleasure in things coming out well.

Hers is an artistic focus. Keeping her sights on the desired finished unit, she zooms in to sample what Brenton is doing, or stands back to contemplate the total dynamics of the group or class. Knowing that the class cannot help her to achieve the proper aesthetic blend if they are unaware of her criteria for valuing, she tells them as a reflective critic what she is making of their work and how she feels about the quality of their involvement and their products.

Her lessons are packed with valuing, almost always positive but with suggestions and prompts: "You could perhaps take one more step. . . ." "If you want to improve it, maybe you could . . . ."

Mrs. Bell isn't coy about her role as judge but her judgment is always in the direction of making her students better judges. To this end, she makes her criteria explicit and does not get into the trickery and sadism we sometimes find in schools where teachers keep the password secret. Behind her connoisseurship is a theory of empowerment. Miss Jean Brodie has no place in her scheme of things.

Conclusion

Putting this all back together again, we are left with the teacher as artist. Her art is to deploy all these roles, and more, flexibly and simultaneously, sometimes with one thing in the front of her consciousness but always with the tonal background of every other item in her repertoire.

She is *poly-attentive*. With one part of her mind's eye on the imagined outcomes, she must read with feeling and sensitivity from the novel, while sensing whether she has engaged the class, knowing how much time she has left and remaining ready to break off for explanation at any time according to a judgement of whether this is necessary or whether it would intrude on the spell of the story. In James Britton's terms she must have both a global and a piecemeal awareness of what is happening. The technician, the scientist and the artist work together.

Frustrating as it may be for teacher educators, I doubt whether we can teach the "feel" that Mrs. Bell has learnt. We can only create the conditions and promote the frame of mind that will allow it to come. I have only been able to construct some fairly crude signposts which point roughly in the direction of that "feel."

When we ask contemporary artists to explain themselves, they refer us back to their work. They are reluctant to translate their effort into words. "If I could tell you what it meant," said Isadora Duncan, "there would be no point in dancing it."

In the end, I cannot translate Mrs. Bell for you. As Frost says: "Poetry is what is lost in the translation."

Perhaps we can illuminate Mrs. Bell's work by noting the difference between synchronized music played by musicians obedient to a strict conductor, and music interweaving rhythm patterns played by improvisors, with their own downbeats.

Certain African musicians carry on five simultaneous rhythms, the melody and four percussions parts. Three rhythms are common in pre-literate music: melody, handclapping and tapping the feet; the individual performs all three simultaneously; though not in synchronization. (This section is taken with alterations from *They Came What They Beheld*, Edmund Carpenter, Outerbridge and Dienstfrey, New York, 1970.)

I suspect that something pre-literate, passionate and primitive pulses behind the civilized surfaces of Mrs. Bell's teaching. Analogies with dance, music and sculpture help us to get closer to what she does. But they are inadequate. It is left for me simply to celebrate her achievement. I hope that we will all recognize in Mrs. Bell the wonder of ourselves. I challenge us all to continue to learn as much as possible about the loom and to weave with imagination.

English Language, English Culture, English Teaching:

A Retrospective on the IFTE Seminar

IAN PRINGLE

Carleton University (Canada)

The ghost of Dartmouth haunts us still.

Until I participated in the 1984 IFTE seminar at East Lansing, Michigan, I believed without question what Aviva Freedman and I wrote in the Preface to *Reinventing the Rhetorical Tradition* (Freedman and Pringle, 1980, p. viii): that whereas the 1966 Dartmouth seminar left its participants with an overwhelming impression of the differences between British and American attitudes to English education—an astonishment on the part of both the British and American delegations that their counterparts could believe what they did and do what they did in the name of English education—at the 1979 international conference, "Learning to Write," one had a much stronger feeling that (at least in the field of rhetoric and composition) there are now strong commonalities which bind us. My assumption that such commonalities hold more broadly in English education was shaken several times at East Lansing.

As a participant in the study group on "Language and Multicultural Education," I had to test my belief that I know what should be done about multiculturalism and multilingualism in the schools both against concepts of multiculturalism that I had never previously considered, and also against sometimes harrowing descriptions by teachers from other parts of the world of multicultural situations which they have to live with on a daily basis—situations which cry out for improvement but for which I can see no possible solution

---

Ian Pringle, incoming Chair of the International Federation for the Teaching of English, delivered the closing address at the IFTE Seminar. This paper is an edited and somewhat extended version of that address prepared for this volume.

119

other than a scale of political action beyond any at which I, as an individual English teacher, might hope to have any effectiveness.

And repeatedly in the conference I saw failures to communicate. For all the fact that we share a common language, a common literary heritage, and in large measure common goals, our words can still fail to connect us. Something as simple as an intense dislike, on the part of academics from one country, of the preferred rhetorical stance of those from another can betray us into a failure to appreciate or even understand the intended message. We are still caught up in our own provincialisms. Provincialism is not necessarily a bad thing, of course. But it will be just as well if we have no illusions about its existence and its effects on us as a profession.

For me there were two undercurrents to the East Lansing seminar. Each might be characterized in terms of people who were not there. The first group of people who were not there, or at least not in any numbers, are those we sometimes refer to as "classroom teachers" or "practising teachers." Admittedly both terms are, in one sense, absurd. They continue one of the least important of the dichotomies that divide our profession. For my own part, I like to feel that what I do when I teach in my own classroom *is* teaching, even if I now do it in a university, and that when I do it I am practising teaching (a responsibility I take very seriously). But there are all sorts of teachers who couldn't come to East Lansing; who perhaps couldn't hope to attend any such professional conference more than once or twice in their professional lives.

I have a vivid memory of a teacher who accosted me on the Carleton University quadrangle during the 1979 "Learning to Write" conference. We had tried to set up the conference in such a way that those we call "practising teachers" would hardly have any option but to hear at least some theoretical presentations. We felt at that particular stage of the development of research and theory in composition and rhetoric, "practising teachers" needed to learn about what was going on in the field; but also we felt that it is vital that researchers observe and test the effects of their claims on "practising teachers." At that moment in the conference, Professor James Kinneavy had just presented his paper synthesizing the commonalities of his, Britton's, Moffett's and D'Angelo's analyses of the function of discourse (1980). For those acquainted with the work of all four theorists it was a very important paper. But the teacher who accosted me could barely contain herself.

"I have to tell someone," she said. "This is the first conference like this I have ever been to, and if I hear one more professor stand up and pontificate about what goes on in my classroom,

I think I will scream. In that last presentation, I wanted to stand up and shout to the other teachers, 'Don't listen to him. He doesn't know what he's talking about! The answer is IN YOURSELVES!' "

I didn't know how I could respond to her. I still don't. I have a great deal of sympathy for the view, rehearsed repeatedly during the IFTE seminar and caught up in the closing statements of the study group on Language and Schooling (see Rathgen and Johnson, this volume, Part II) that there can be no advance in the English teaching profession unless teachers themselves exert professional control over what is is that happens in English classrooms, and surely this teacher's anger was an assertion of that very claim. But I am myself involved in teacher education; I believe just as firmly that the control teachers exercise in their classrooms cannot truly be professional unless they are conversant with relevant theory. This teacher's reaction demonstrated that she was not in a position to see any relevance for herself in what Kinneavy had been saying, even though I had hoped that the implications of what he was saying would have (as indeed they were already having) dramatic effects on the teaching of composition in North American schools. The gulf between her fury and my hopes is like the gulf between the kinds of statements made at the IFTE seminar about the role we must accord to classroom teachers when we discuss what English education should be and the absence of all but a few such teachers from those very discussions. For me this gulf epitomises what I think is one of the most serious challenges facing our profession as we move towards the third decade since Dartmouth.

What we have discovered since 1966 is phenomenal. We have come to new understandings, especially about the importance of talking and writing, about the development of writing ability, about the beginning of reading and about response to literature—discoveries which, I think, go far beyond what anyone could have predicted or hoped for in 1966. And yet, we still have much to learn about all these topics, and many more. Despite the magnitude of the gains, it is astonishing what we still don't know. Consider, for example, those aspects of classroom discourse which Frances Christie revealed to us in her IFTE plenary address, printed above. How much more of what goes on when we teach remains to be uncovered? And what about all the other questions raised by that paper: how much do teachers need to know, *explicitly*, if they are to teach effectively? Or that other question, raised by Nancy Martin: What about the danger that, if we begin to tell teachers about these things, they'll end up teaching some of them as content, just as some have already begun to teach story grammar as content (and even, in some cases, to test it), and just as others still teach about English grammar?

In some ways, I think the grammar question is central, if only for its symbolic value. On the one hand, despite all the work that has been done on language development since 1966, we still have only very vague ideas of the grammatical resources children can bring to bear on particular tasks, of what the range of possibilities is and what the constraints on that range are, of how the range of possibilities changes developmentally. And on the other hand, the constant repetition by experts and curriculum planners of the advice not to , teach grammar has scarcely touched the practice of most teachers, who continue to do the one thing that has been constant in English teaching since the eighteenth century. The profession is certainly in a position now to review and affirm what we have established about the importance of the productive uses of language, of talking and writing, in the cognitive and social development of our students (and ourselves); and also to review and, I think, to extend, our understandings of how those abilities develop, how they can be fostered in our classrooms. But there is also much that remains to be done of the enterprise we set out on with Dartmouth.

There are also parts of those achievements that we need to review. For one thing, I think we need to look once again at the opposition between the view of English which sees English as something we give to students, and the view that our task as English teachers is to explore with our students the range of their experience (certainly their life experience, but also, one hopes, their literary experience), and to help them to bring those experiences to articulate expression. I think the latter is, roughly, the "Growth through English" model, best known through John Dixon's book of that name which was his own account of and reflection on Dartmouth. In the plenary sessions at the IFTE seminar, it was twice described as a "romantic" and "idealistic" model. Such a view is becoming more and more familiar. Perhaps it is a direct consequence of the conservative temper so characteristic of Britain, like the U.S. and Canada in the 1980s. It perturbs me that people in IFTE should seem to countenance such a view: as though our failure to succeed when we aim very high means that it is wrong to do so; that we must be more "realistic" and keep closer to what is the present norm. For my own part, if the vision of English expressed by James Moffett and John Dixon in their plenary addresses is romantic, then, as an English teacher, that is what I want to be too.

In addition to reviewing the opposition between English as something given to students and English as something done together with students, I think as well that we may need to look some more at reading, at the relationships between reading and writing, and between reading and what others call the teaching of English literature. I think we need to look especially at the great gulf which continues to separate what goes on in many university English departments from the rest of what is called English education. After all, if a journalist wants an expert opinion on some aspect of English education, he or she will almost certainly go to a university English department to find the expert. It seems obvious to almost everybody else that this is where one can find the experts on what we do. That is not our view. I think in large measure we share a view that people in university English departments in the first place do not know what we do, do not know why we do it, know too little about the research and theory which justify our attempts, and thus generally marginalize our relevance to their own work. Perhaps in retaliation, we tend to belittle them, regarding their work as an esoteric game with little relevance to what we do.

It may be that this gulf is in reality a symptom or demonstration of something fundamental that has happened: perhaps the kind of academic study of literature which is the predominant activity of university English departments has moved so far from our concerns that there are now two distinct and unrelated fields, whose common name "English" is merely the consequence of a series of historical accidents. Is there any other explanation of the difference between the study of literature in university English departments and the concept of literature to be seen in the report of the "Language and Human Values" study group (See Part II, below)? And yet we know that almost all those who currently participate in "English," as it is currently understood, do at least share a fundamental commitment to and love of literature in English; there is at least still that to bind us. Is there anything more?

Beyond those aspects of our discipline that we need to review, one of the strongest currents of thought and feeling in the IFTE seminar was the sense that we need to stop, to take stock, to reflect on what we missed as the profession developed after Dartmouth (for there are certainly things we missed), on what went wrong (for some things certainly went wrong), as well as on what we gained and what we have left unresolved. For, like many of the participants, I have a sense that the gains since Dartmouth are terribly tenuous; that, at least in Canada, the U.S. and Britain, political forces are operating in ways that jeopardize almost all the gains of the last twenty years. This is perhaps too pessimistic a view. For me, it is certainly coloured by my awareness of what was going on in Ontario prior to the IFTE conference. Let me give two examples:

A few weeks before the East Lansing meeting, I was invited to give a workshop for a school board in southwestern Ontario. As I began to ask the organizers what they wanted, it became clear to me what they had in mind for this professional day which was to launch their "new thrust" to increase the amount and kind of writing done in their system. It was to begin with a 1½ hour session in which people from the board's program department would summarize for the teachers the insights they themselves had gained by reading material put out by the Ministry, encapsulated in a few key slogans displayed on overheads. This would be followed by keynote addresses by outside experts—people known to be good solid talkers who can also be entertaining. And then, after lunch, in a parallel session with a number of other workshop leaders, I was to give a 2½ hour workshop on "Revising and Editing." Almost every assumption they had brought to the task of organising the "new thrust" ran completely counter to everything I believe I know about how such a "new thrust" might be implemented effectively—and this, not in some distant northern wilderness, but in a southern urban area within easy driving distance of East Lansing; in a jurisdiction whose teachers could easily have had access to nearby workshops given annually for several years by Donald Graves and Mary Ellen Giacobbe; a jurisdiction which could have taken advantage of all the work done in this area by the Ontario Council of Teachers of English, the Canadian Council of Teachers of English, the Ontario Ministry of Education. Obviously I am singling out one example. But I do it because my experience with this particular board is so typical of so much of what I see in in-service work with teachers.

My second example is a colloquium I participated in, the week before the Seminar. It was organised in part by the Curriculum Division of the Ontario Ministry of Education. In Ontario, we have had no Province-wide assessment of English since 1968, but the political pressure to restore examinations is very strong. The colloquium had been planned by the Curriculum Branch of the Ministry to promote, in the place of exams, the use of writing folders as a means of English assessment. It became clear to me during the colloquium (not least because it was perfectly explicit) that the Evaluation Branch of the Ministry, while it didn't really care whether the Curriculum Branch gets its writing folders or not, was determined that we will have two other kinds of evaluation: one, an in-class writing assignment on an assigned topic; and the other a machine-scoreable test of language skills. It's easy to suggest that the kinds of English teachers conjured up in Robert Pattison's paper are mere straw men. For my own part

I would want to stress that, behind the stereotypes he works with, behind the caricatures he evokes for us, there *is* a reality, and one whose existence we must not ignore.

One of the things we must reflect on most urgently is why we have failed to convince those in political power that we have actually been working towards what I think are ultimately the very goals they want us to achieve, even if we have been doing it in ways different from the ways they expect. (Why not? We have found ways of doing it better.) Why is it that, in the face of so many gains that seem so clear to us, people still perceive literacy crises? Even more urgently, why have we failed to touch the practice of all but a very small minority of teachers? I was immensely encouraged by what we learned at the IFTE Seminar about recent developments in Australia and, especially, in New Zealand; I would agree, too (though with some qualifications), that in the U.S. the National Writing Project provides us with a valuable model of implementation. But against these gains I would set once again that other reality: that all across Canada and the United States, at all levels of English education, people continue to teach, as content, an analysis of English grammar whose vacuousness was first pointed out by William Cobbett at the beginning of the nineteenth century. The grammar issue is indeed symbolic. Why is it that unjustifiable content and bad pedagogy persist so strongly in the face of what we now know? What went wrong with implementation? What else do we need to know about working with teachers?

Such concerns as these strike me as I reflect on those "practising teachers" who, symptomatically, were not at the IFTE seminar. In a way, they challenge the claim we might otherwise feel entitled to articulate that we are at the forefront of the profession. Perhaps we too are on the periphery.

The other group who were not there challenge the very idea that there is such a profession.

On the whole, we anglophones have become quite comfortable with the idea that the language we call "English" has, for most of us, only a historical connection with England. Admittedly there are still some who don't share that view. By coincidence, I shared the taxi I took through the tunnel from Windsor, Ontario, to Detroit, Michigan, on my way to the IFTE seminar, with a lugubrious Englishman whose accent revealed to me that he was a native of Birmingham, but who told me that he had spent a good part of his adult life in New Zealand. He was delighted to learn that I was going to an international conference of English teachers, and asked me to pass on to the New Zealand teachers present the message that they should start teaching English in schools again. "And you too," he added. "You don't even speak English any longer; you all speak American."

In our profession, such provincialism is, happily, increasingly rare. We acknowledge that, despite the minor differences we notice, we all speak a common language. But in fact, once one admits that the English language is no longer exclusively the language of the English, it is remarkably hard to determine exactly what English really is. It's striking that, shortly before the conference, a number of publishers independently produced books dealing with national varieties of English other than those of the major English-speaking countries: Bailey and Görlach's *English as a World Language*; Pride's *New Englishes*; Loreto Todd's *Modern Englishes, Pidgins and Creoles*. Under the general editorship of Professor Manfred Görlach, John Benjamin's in Holland have launched a series of books called "Varieties of English Around the World;" in the U.S., Pergamon Press have launched another series called "English in the International Context," under the general editorship of Professor Braj Kachru.

It is just over four hundred years since Elizabeth I issued to Sir Humphrey Gilbert the letters patent which authorized the foundation of the first English colony outside of Britain, in Newfoundland, and thus began the spread of English around the world. And it is now two hundred years since the first moves to assert the independent validity of American English set us on the path towards our generally relaxed recognition today that the varieties of English in the major English-speaking countries have just as much right to call themselves English as the English of England. Before our very eyes, another such movement is beginning to assert that a large number of other varieties of English spoken in countries where English is in some sense an official language, but hardly ever a first language, can lay an equal claim to validity and independence. If, today, we set out to describe the English language, we are forced to deal with the fact that it includes not only the international edited standard written English of this text, but conceivably the English-based creoles of the Solomon Islands, Cameroon, New Guinea, and Ghana, and certainly most of the other varieties in the long continuum which joins those two extremes.

But if this is what the English language is, what then is "English culture"? We are used to dealing with the concept of culture in two senses. One is high culture, of which, for us, English literature is a very important part; some of us, indeed, still think we have a duty to pass it on, in English courses at various levels. The other perception, which we gained originally from the work of such people as Franz Boas and Edward Sapir, as they sought to make us understand how it would feel to be a Hopi or a Shawnee, is that culture is a static set of assumptions and values possessed (usually) by other peoples.

The reality, of course, is that our relation to our common "English culture," whatever that is, is first a transaction, in much the same way as our interaction with a literary text is a transaction. Just as our encounter with any text will depend on what we bring to it at a particular time, so too we may talk about our culture as though it were something static, external, equally accessible in principle to us all. But in reality what we experience of it is determined by what we ourselves bring (which means what we ourselves are) at any particular time.

There is also a difference, however, between our experience of a literary text and our experience of our culture. In a trivial but real sense, texts do have some physical existence outside of our aesthetic experience of them. It's possible, for example, to weigh them, or count the words in them, or gather them together in heaps and burn them. Cultures, on the other hand, have no existence beyond the potential and current participation in them of all those who have some access to them at one particular time. For *all* of us, that access can only be limited, and partial. When my nine-year-old son, who really is French-speaking, and whose English is very superficial, but whose grade 5 English teacher, for reasons I'd rather not speculate on (though I suspect incompetence, and sheer stupidity), wanted him to read Judy Blume's *Are You There, God? It's Me, Margaret*, and we discussed that, he and I; or when my 16-year-old son (who elected to switch out of the French language system and take his secondary education in English) asked me, as he did a short time ago, if I would get out of the university library a book summarizing the plot of *The Merry Wives of Windsor*, because he was studying it in English, and found he didn't have time to read it, and we discussed *that*; then, in both cases, what English culture could be to my sons changed by virtue of our common participation in those aspects of it. The very attempt to characterize English culture confronts one with the kind of paradox familiar in sociolinguistic research. The task of the sociolinguistic researcher is to try to describe how language works when its users are not being observed; however, the only way to do this is to observe them, and the very fact of observation can change performance.

To observe means to participate, and to participate means to change. English culture is not, and cannot be, one; and what is more, it is not, and cannot be, stable. What we work with and in, as English teachers, is not English culture, but English cultures, and English cultures are always in a state of becoming. And so too our individual experiences of them are tentative transactions.

To some extent they are cumulative. My discussions with my sons are, I hope, not as enlarging an experience for me as I want them to be for them, because I've often participated in similar opportunities which our cultures make available to us. But my participation, like theirs, is still tentative; like theirs, my total perception at any time of what English culture might be is always limited. Our lives are a series of acculturations into new ranges of what is possible for us culturally: from the child's first acculturation, by learning English, into the English culture of the home; the extension of that, also mediated largely by language, into the broader cultural ranges of the immediate community, and then the special sub-cultures of the nursery school and the school itself; the subsequent acculturation into the possibilities of literacy; and so on, through increasingly broader interactions with parts of the developing whole including, for some, the kind of acculturation that may come with pre-service and in-service teacher training, and so on.

In all of this, you will note, I continue to assume that English is a language and has cultures which are acquired by those whose environment is English-speaking, and I have been envisioning a kind of language, and therefore a set of cultural possibilities, which are, in a sense, inherited by virtue of the fact that English is "the first language." A multiple ambiguity, that: the second first language in the world is also the first second language.

The other group of people who weren't at IFTE were, first, the vast numbers of people for whom English is a first language, in places like the Caribbean, some Pacific Islands, parts of Africa, and many parts of our own countries, where those who speak it differ from us, in many cases, by the colour of their skin, but in some cases also because they feel that what we think English culture is for us can only be external to them, and is to be rejected. And then there are the even vaster numbers of people for whom English is acquired, in some ways, as an external language, acquired later than the mother tongue, perhaps in communities where English has only a very narrowly restricted domain.

What, today, is English culture? It isn't only the range of cultural participation possible for anglophone monolinguals in countries like Canada, Australia, New Zealand, England, the U.S., including those elements of those societies who are most marginalized, most inclined to reject what they perceive to be our enterprise. It is also the cultural potential of bilinguals in those countries who are of indigenous origin, the Maori, the Aborigines, the Amerindians, the Inuit, who suffered colonization by our ancestors. It is also the cultural potential of the bilinguals who are the inheritors of an earlier wave of European colonists, like the Hispanics in the U.S., the French in Canada, and even the Celts in Britain, and that of all the recent immigrants who have maintained another language. It is also the cultural potential offered by those new Englishes groping towards standardization in places like Nigeria, India, Singapore, Fiji, where English is a national language, but not a first language. And it is even the cultural potential offered by the school English of places like Denmark (which has seen some very interesting work recently on oracy in English at the intermediate level) or the Philippines, a nation of some 50 million people for whom English is the normal language of secondary education. English is no longer only English; it is also English as a second language, and English as a foreign language. We have before us, as a profession, the immense task of getting it right about bilingualism and, I would add, getting it right about multiculturalism—of doing whatever we can to ensure that, for those for whom English seems, from our perspective, "external," it will still be something that fosters the cognitive, communicative and personal potentialities of their children in just the same way as I hope it will for my own children.

Some of the questions raised by that claim are perhaps only trivialities. I remember reading in the *Times Literary Supplement* over twenty years ago a letter in which some Englishman was complaining about the response of a visiting African postgraduate student to a drive in the country one spring. The visitor had seen, for the first time in his life, a crowd, a host, of certain yellow flowers, and was moved to recite from memory Wordsworth's "Daffodils." The trouble was that the flowers he had seen were actually dandelions. The letter writer, as I remember it, was very angry about this situation; I think he felt that some part of the culture he had inherited by right as a native speaker of English was being alienated from him by the participation of others who hadn't inherited it by birth, or at least not through the mother tongue.

Such provincialism, I'm sure, is today even rarer than the kind of provincialism which would insist that only the English (even, perhaps, only the English of Birmingham) actually speak English. But it might still be worth asking ourselves just how much validity we are willing to accord to a Vietnamese refugee child's transaction with a poem by Walt Whitman, say, or a Nigerian high school student's reading of a poem by John Donne, or the view of the canon of English literature held by an Indian child whose teacher's views of English literature were determined almost entirely by his preparation for Cambridge "O" levels a generation and a half ago (compare Nagarajan 1981). And on the other hand, we must in all honesty ask ourselves what kind of legitimacy we can grant to our own reading of a novel written in English by a Nigerian novelist such as Chinua Achebe, who has chosen English as the medium of his literary expression—but clearly the English of Nigeria; or for that matter, our reading of a lyric poem by the bilingual and bicultural New Zealand poet Hone Tuwhare, able to represent in English echoes of a Polynesian experience which to most of us is permanently alien.

At the time of the IFTE seminar I had two groups of students in my classes who had been sent to Canada from elsewhere to learn something of what we think English teaching might be. One was a group of three visiting scholars from the People's Republic of China. They were English teachers before they came, and would be English teachers when they returned. They seemed to me to be baffled, at every moment, by Canada and Canadian English. I don't think I have ever encountered a group of people with whom I could share fewer commonalities. Yet, to an outsider, we are all English teachers. The other was a group of about twenty students from Malaysia. A few of them were native speakers of Tamil, Fukkien and Mandarin, and these therefore were trilingual in their first language, Bahasa Melayu and English. The others were native speakers of Bahasa Melayu, and were thus bilingual. All of them had received instruction in English, as subject, at the secondary level, and all had a very impressive command of English, though an English far removed from mine, and one which, at times, I felt was very alien. They weren't yet English teachers, but when they returned they would be, for their country has defined English as one of its national languages, with a particular role to play in its overall educational system.

The final challenge which I would draw from the uneasy undercurrents of feeling I sensed at East Lansing is not a retrospect on what has been happening to the profession in our countries in the twenty years since Dartmouth. It is rather a prospect for the future of English teaching as a profession. Thanks to the increasing numbers of non-native speakers of English in our own classes, we have no choice today but to acknowledge that what we used to call English belongs as well to those whose mother tongue is some other language. Our challenge is to accept the logical consequences of that recognition. We must recognize that English as language is not only the varieties spoken by us in our own countries, but all varieties, that English as subject is still our subject wherever it is taught.

There are, I think, immediate advantages to us in such a recognition. I have argued elsewhere (1984) that we stand to benefit from looking closely at the implications for our own field of recent work in E.S.L. But even if there were no such prospect of benefits for us, it still seems to me to be the case that the International Federation for the Teaching of English can no longer accept the limits inherited inadvertently from earlier, narrower concepts of what it is to be an English teacher.

REFERENCES

Bailey, R. W. and Görlach, M. (1982) *English as a World Language.* Ann Arbor: University of Michigan Press.

Dixon, J. (1967). *Growth Through English.* London: Oxford University Press.

Freedman, A. and Pringle, I., eds. (1980). *Reinventing the Rhetorical Tradition.* Conway, AR: L & S Books, for the CCTE.

Kinneavy, J. (1980). A pluralistic synthesis of four contemporary models for teaching composition. In Freedman, A., and Pringle, I., eds. *Reinventing the Rhetorical Tradition* (Conway, AR: L & S Books, for the CCTE), pp. 37-52.

Nagarajan, S. (1981). The decline of English in India: Some historical notes. *College English 43*, 7, pp. 663-670.

Pride, J. B., ed. (1982). *New Englishes.* Rowley, MA, London and Tokyo: Newbury House.

Pringle, I. (1984). English as a world language—right out there in the playground. In Arnold, R., ed. *Timely Voices* (Melbourne and London: Oxford University Press), pp. 187-208.

Todd, L. (1984). *Modern Englishes: Pidgins and Creoles.* Oxford: Basil Blackwell.

Part II

Global Imperatives for Literacy and Learning in English

Study group reports from the Seminar of the International Federation for the Teaching of English, November 11–14, 1984.

Study Group 1:
Language, Politics, and Public Affairs

Chair:
JOHN DIXON
(U.K.)

"Politics means power," said a class of high school students in Melbourne. How did they come to think that? They had been bored with their English textbook and, rather to their surprise, when "someone suggested we should write our own book . . . we never looked back." In fact, they ended up publishing it (AE Press, 1982). What is more, after starting with sections on *School, Smoking* and *Hanging Around*—these were *not* students on a university track—they finally moved on into *Politics, Nuclear War, The Future* and *"World, here we Come!"* So they began to ask fundamental questions: "Who has the power? . . . How can that power be transferred? Whose interests does the power serve? . . ." In doing so, they "started to run the class," as their teachers acknowledged.

Here, then, in a political microcosm—their own school—students were learning to claim and earn democratic power. And, in winning access to it, they realised that democratic power depends crucially on language. Decisions had to be made. Negotiation was essential. Other people's backing and interest had to be enlisted. A wider public had to be persuaded and convinced, their needs considered, their questions answered. All these things depend on language used with care, precision and political acumen.

Moving up through the many levels of political power in our countries, the same lessons apply. In the school or university council, in the school board or education committee, in the local press or media, in provincial and state ministries, in national or multi-national corporations (including those controlling Press and Television), in the federal and national governments—at all these levels, language is the key. Political struggles over the decisions to be made are necessarily carried on through language. Thus, language (together with visuals) is increasingly used to enlist popular support and to create a constituency of people whose views fit those of the decision-makers.

How well is such language used in 1984, and in whose interests? Aye, there's the rub. In our societies, economic power brings easy access to political control. And delegated power in our "democracies" often gives power to the few over the many. As a result of these two entrenched factors, people with economic and political power all too often abuse language. On occasion they cover up or lie; more often they tend to promulgate a distorted view of reality, a smokescreen behind which they are free to operate. George Orwell may have been wrong in many of his prophecies about 1984, but he was not so wide of the mark over Doublespeak and Doublethink.

As teachers of English, then, we have some searching questions to face. What responsibilities inevitably fall on us, both within the profession and within our own subject? What should we be studying, learning and teaching about the language of politics?

The IFTE study group on "Language, Politics, and Public Affairs" proposed three directions for investigation:

a. How does the curriculum prepare students to use the full range of language they need to take their part in public affairs—in school and beyond?
b. How does the curriculum prepare students to recognise and critically analyse the full range of language used in political life?
c. Since analysis and use of political language necessarily raise ethical questions, how does the curriculum prepare students to make their own ethical decisions?

These are the questions we want to put to our five national associations and, through them, to all interested colleagues. What kinds of action do we foresee?

First, it would be valuable to have national collections of case studies, showing how students from school through university have learnt to take an informed part in public affairs at various levels. Betsy Kaufman's seminar paper (See Appendix B.) described an episode at Queens College (U.S.A.) which demonstrated positively and negatively how much stands to be learnt in student politics. During the seminar there were many other stories, too, of school or college students who had taken their democratic responsibilities seriously. What are they learning—and what education are they getting—about democratic uses of power? How self-critical can they become about their own use of language in the public domain? English teachers throughout the world need examples to inspire them and to demonstrate how students can progress from small beginnings to wider public issues, with all the complex uses of thought and language these demand.

Second, we strongly recommend to readers throughout the world the initiative already taken by the National Council of Teachers of English (U.S.A.) in its studies of the language of advertising, political commentators, candidates for political office and all those who transmit through the public media. This has taken four forms:

a. the setting up of a standing committee on Public Doublespeak;
b. the publication of two major books, *Language and Public Policy* (Rank, 1974) and *Teaching about Doublespeak* (Dieterich, 1978);
c. the steady development of teaching materials, supported by the *Quarterly Review of Doublespeak*;
d. two annual awards, the Orwell Award for "an outstanding contribution to the critical analysis of public discourse" and the Doublespeak "tribute" to "American public figures who have perpetrated language that is grossly deceptive, evasive, euphemistic, confusing or self-contradictory . . . with pernicious social or political consequences."

There was a close-run decision on the Orwell Award for 1984 between Lt. Col. Thomas Murawski "for his pioneering efforts to combat governmentese through a Plain English course" and Ted Koppel, moderator of ABC-TV's *Nightline*, who offered "a model of intelligence, informed interest, social awareness, verbal fluency, with fair and rigorous questioning" (Lutz, 1984). The Doublespeak Award went to U.S. President Ronald Reagan for the following statement to a Central American national assembly: "Any nation destabilizing its neighbours by protecting guerrillas and exporting violence should forfeit close and fruitful relations with any people who truly love peace and freedom." Peter Evans's seminar paper, "Language, Politics and the News" (Appendix B), reminds us that politicians outside the U.S.A. are just as guilty of public doublespeak.

There is already a rich source, then, of ideas and experience in analysing the political use and abuse of language. Moreover, through critically analysing the language of politics, high and low, students can earn the right to make their own "awards" and to join in the campaign to eradicate the abuses that most concern them. In doing so they start to become the active citizens needed in order to extend democracy in the face of forces Orwell recognized too well.

Politics and Spoken English

Every day Doublespeak and Doublethink are used to undermine the democratic base of our societies, making the struggle to
maintain it that much harder. Equally, though public awareness and
scepticism are rising, many arguments and campaigns over the use of
the English language are being diverted—no doubt to the relief of
double-speakers—into crassly false directions. Such diversionary campaigns prey on and boost common prejudices about the superiority
of "English," or certain prestige forms of it, over other languages and
cultures.

Bigotry over the way people speak (or look, or dress) must be
nearly as old as speech itself. Nevertheless, in political, economic
and cultural "empires" it is organised in specially obnoxious ways.
To the cultural imperialist of whatever kind, "colonial" dialects are
necessarily inferior, as Australians and New Zealanders can testify
to this day. Where the dialect is identified with race, as in Africa or
India, and additionally with former slavery, as in the West Indies, the
stench of prejudice rises higher.

Most people find it hard to resist the self-flattery that their
speech is somehow better than others'. This is rich muck for dema-
gogues to rake in, and a secret source for those who rationalise their
distaste (not too well) by arguing about maintaining "the purity of
the language." In the face of their (self-)deceit, evasions and confu-
sions, it is more than usually important to be plain about the real
issue: how to help speakers of various dialects of the same language
to make clear their meanings to each other, without unintentionally
raising difficulties or giving offence.

The answer, when you think seriously about it, is not a single
"standard" for spoken English to which everybody defers, for who
would define it—American, Australian, Canadian, English, Irish, New
Zealand, or Scots speakers (to go no further than current IFTE members)? Rather it consists of modifications within each major dialect
that make oral comprehension easy across regional and national
frontiers. These modifications are being worked out right now, in
face-to-face conversation and—often very influentially—on television.
No one, it turns out, need set his or her face against the accent of
social class or ethnic group or region, but all have to learn to make
accommodations. And with good will this is happening, in school
and beyond.

The IFTE study group therefore put forward a Bill of Rights
for all students speaking the English language:

The students of English around the world are a richly diverse
and rapidly expanding group. Though the clientele of English

instruction has perhaps always been more heterogeneous than teachers or curriculum-makers have acknowledged, the fact remains that recent patterns of migration and social change have greatly multiplied the kinds of pupils studying English. Our five countries enroll perhaps only one-fifth of the world's population of English students; nevertheless, even our students represent a huge range of racial, ethnic, geographical, religious, social class, and linguistic differences.

Given this diversity and complexity, it seems important that we English teachers affirm:

1. That we accept our students' right to the varieties of language they bring to school. We appreciate that all varieties of language fulfil common human purposes in their home speech communities; we embrace and celebrate the richness of this variation.
2. That one—but only one—of the English teacher's jobs is to help students add to their speech repertoire a variant of their dialect of English that is usable as a *lingua franca.*
3. That English teachers must also teach *about* language. We should teach about how language is used (and abused) in real social contexts, including why prestige dialects exist and how they are perpetuated.

Politics and an International Campaign for Literacy

In our five countries, the inescapable fact of the last decade has been the failure of the "West" to sustain economic growth, full employment and prosperity. For something close to a majority of our fellow-citizens—and for hundreds of millions in the Third World—the economic system is working against them. Many others are hanging on nervously to the gains of the past, unsure about the future.

It is a difficult time to be far-sighted and to keep one's political nerve. Much easier, indeed, to manufacture a crisis where there is none, to whip up public apprehensions and ride to personal accolades on the back of a frantic, mass desire for security. Thus, as Harvey Daniels correctly guesses in his seminar paper, "The Literacy Crisis That Wouldn't Die" (Appendix B), that like the U.S.A., most of our countries have recently suffered "Education Crises" and within them "Literacy Crises." Let us admit that for the demagogue, teachers are easy game; like the sinner, the average teacher is only too ready to believe he or she could do better. Nevertheless, when faced by political attacks on education for its "failures," we would do well to reiterate the crucial question: *Who, then, is responsible for the continuing economic failure of the "West"?* Until that is effectively answered, and the harsh economic realities reversed, what right have politicians in power to criticise *us?* Equally, however, teachers and their national associations have themselves to blame if they remain on the defensive forever, and allow "crisis" campaigners to flood the media with prophetic Cassandras, wildly confident that English is on the decline —nay, terminally ill—and that the nation (excluding the speaker) is being overwhelmed by "a rising tide of mediocrity." It is time that the five IFTE associations took the initiative, linked up with their colleagues, and launched a positive campaign for literacy.

By a historical irony, the fact is that over the last decade, the hope for average students, the knowledge of their potential as users of language, has grown from strength to strength. Within our countries, projects on writing or reading—strongly supported by our national associations—have demonstrated what average students and their teacher can achieve, working together with the right kind of support. And the message is beginning to get through. Allen Berger and Regina Rattigan's paper, "What Do Governors and Educators Recommend . . .?" (Appendix B), quotes a state governor who explicitly recognises the need "to support a system of teacher-as-researcher and teacher-teaching-teacher" as a prime mover in any campaign to improve reading and writing.

The study group spent much of its time, therefore, considering how best to seize the political initiative. It finally drew up a set of brief guidelines in three parts.

We put these proposals forward now as a basis for discussion and action. They are intended not merely for the executive boards of our five associations but also for all readers who believe that in the present political climate what both students and teachers need most of all is to have positive targets for the future, and a practical hope that these can be achieved.

I. Principles and Beliefs

- Everyone has the right to be literate.

- Societies in the major English-speaking countries have the means to make literacy possible for all citizens, and to help others in the Third World to do so.

- The attainment of literacy is a complex process that requires a continuing quest for knowledge through research based on the experience of teachers and learners. (Searching to identify problems and discover solutions is made quite difficult by the enormous diversity of issues and factors related to illiteracy.)

- The effects of illiteracy on people of the world have been disastrous, affecting the quality of life.

- Countries must establish both local and national commitments to literacy programs—commitments which rise above current interests and funding practices of public and private agencies. Funding to advance literacy requires a long-term commitment.

II. General Recommendations

Universal literacy is best achieved through a concerted and continuing effort on the part of IFTE organisations:

a. to translate their deliberations and stances into public policies;
b. to educate publics and governments of IFTE member nations to use their resources most effectively;
c. to establish public policy committees or commissions within each of the IFTE member organisations.

The IFTE itself should seek to assist member organisations by:

1. educating public policy-makers, legislators and other educational organisations;
2. serving as a clearing-house for collecting and disseminating knowledge about literacy;
3. providing a forum for the free and open exchange of ideas relating to literacy;
4. seeking funds to establish an international action centre for the advancement of literacy;
5. establishing an international institute for faculty development;
6. supporting continued action research on literacy;
7. making the case for both private and public support;
8. identifying needs as well as ways of meeting needs;
9. convincing the private sector of the need for both seed money and ongoing funding;
10. examining in-service education models such as the U.S. National Writing Project, as potential vehicles for improving literacy;
11. linking up with other countries, especially those of the Third World where English is of prime importance.

III. Specific Campaign Strategies

- Establish a committee charged with documenting and publicising successful projects, including details about the procedures used.

- Identify policy-making committees and seek representation on them (e.g. research and planning commissions of State Boards of Education).

- Support—and get strong representation on—parent-teacher organisations.

- Organise teacher-support groups on the local level.

- Develop local projects that entail parent involvement (e.g. parent-child activity calendars, procedures for parents participating in developing school curricula).

- Develop local projects that have visibility (e.g. annual Young Writers' Workshops).

- Identify very precisely projects that will deservedly gain media attention because they are news and they meet the needs of the community (e.g. schoolkids being pen-pals with residents of nursing homes).

- Identify other ways of gaining media visibility (e.g. preparing press releases, pushing for an Education Page in local newspapers, using cable access channels).

- Have a media representative on each organisation committee.

In putting forward these proposals, our study group had the following political advice to give itself and all like-minded colleagues: determine whether and where your organisation lacks credibility and power; identify the causes. Define the forces that militate against change, including economic self-interest, political realities, and questionable assumptions about language and literacy.

Convince those you wish to influence that they have a problem which your proposals will help them to solve. Make face-to-face contact with them. Expand your focus beyond the schools to the under-literate adult population and to the relationship of literacy to the quality of life.

Identify specific targets and concentrate on one target at a time.

Through publicity and other means, establish ways of rewarding people and projects that are successful in advancing your aims. Use ordinary language and vivid metaphor when talking to anyone outside our organisations. Operate confidently, not defensively, knowing that ours is an important profession.

The Politics of Testing and Assessment

Testing is a political act; it involves the use of power. Who holds the power today, and whose interests are they serving? The most powerful single group in most of our countries are the "competency" testing agencies or the examination boards. In effect, they are the "experts" who decide what is valued in English and thus what is taught.

We can demonstrate that, so far as English is concerned, this power is open to serious abuse in the following ways:

a. Key principles of language and learning have been thrashed out in theory and practice over the past two decades. Most tests are being designed contrary to these principles.

b. Timed tests inevitably narrow the range of reading covered, distort writing in the process of testing it, and frequently omit speaking and listening altogether (not to mention studies of language, television and drama).

c. Mass tests are inevitably biased against minority and underprivileged groups; they minimise and often neglect language achievements within ethnic cultures, and give a low priority to the experience of women and disadvantaged groups.

The content of most tests and examinations, then, will not stand up to serious criticism on educational grounds. But in terms of political responsibility the testing boards are open to further and equally serious criticism:

d. Students, parents and teachers want to know what the individual student can achieve in English with the help of a given course of study. Tests in the main make no statements about achievements; they are designed to give the student a rank order, that is all.

e. Although tests inevitably decide what is valued and taught, testing agencies have no claim to special knowledge or expertise in curriculum matters, nor in teaching and learning. In other words, they are being given responsibilities which they cannot discharge.

It is on these grounds that several states and provinces have already decided to pilot a new basis for assessment. This includes:

i. the assembly of a sample of the student's optimum achievements over the course of a year or more (e.g. a writing folder);
ii. a concise, formative description of those achievements and the progress that has been made;
iii. self-evaluating comments made by the students and their peers;
iv. further evaluative comments from parents and other "real audiences" who have read or heard the students' work;
v. teacher meetings, where these materials can be analysed and discussed, so that common standards can be established (with published exemplars) for a local area, province or state;
vi. through such meetings, external moderation for the individual English department's assessments.

In any campaign for literacy, then, IFTE members will need to give priority to replacing competency testing and similar agencies by systems of assessment which are open to public inspection, formative and designed to describe what students are achieving.

REFERENCES

AE Press, Students of 10E, Albert Park High School (1982). Move over teacher. Melbourne.

Dieterich, D., ed. (1978). *Teaching about Doublespeak*. Urbana, Illinois: National Council of Teachers of English.

Lutz, W. (1984). Presentation speech for the Orwell and Doublespeak Awards. Detroit.

Rank, H., ed. (1974). *Language and Public Policy*. Urbana: NCTE.

Study Group 2:
Language and Schooling

Chairs:

ELODY RATHGEN
Christchurch Girls High School (N.Z.)

FRED JOHNSON
Papanui High School (N.Z.)

Frances Christie, consultant to the Language and Schooling study group, developed in her plenary address to the IFTE Seminar the idea that language learning is the hidden curriculum of our schooling. Success within the school system is very often a matter of mastering a particular pattern or genre of language. Children may have content, cognitive skills, interest, even experience, but unless they acquire the language patterns valued by the schools, they are likely to be assessed as failures. Instead of allowing language to be a creative resource reflecting the individuality of a learner, schools have made it a basis for measurement and established a hierarchy of language genres.

Any attempt to change these accepted patterns of "school" language and our present systems of assessment which are based on them could have far reaching consequences. As James Moffett said in his plenary address, "The Hidden Impediment," both administrators and lay people in power within the school and education systems have a vested interest in *not* encouraging changes in language learning. Teachers therefore have a very important role: many know, in theory, a good deal more about language teaching than they put into practice. Perhaps political and social pressures inhibit them. Only when teachers believe in the need for change and are committed to working for it will we see students enfranchised rather than inhibited by the language teaching within our schools.

The Working Process of the Study Group

The study group first met to identify areas of common concern, then attempted to break down the topic, "Language and Schooling," into more specific issues which could be discussed in smaller groups. The background papers prepared by participants and the contributions of the two consultants helped the group establish four main issues:

—What is the present status of the *personal growth* model of language acquisition?
—What does the teacher need to know about language learning and teaching, and what is the teacher's relationship and responsibility to society outside of the school?
—How is change in schooling and language learning brought about?
—What will be the political consequence of change, and what strategies need to be worked out in order to achieve them?

The Study Group Report

Position Statements

1. The status of the language growth model.

i. The personal growth model of language development is under pressure in IFTE member countries for the following reasons:
—political and economic pressures, leading to
—standardization of the curriculum;
—a preoccupation with so-called "basic skills," and
—an overemphasis upon testing, with
—a wash-back effect upon the curriculum, leading to teaching for testing and assessment.

ii. That the model is effective is attested to by some outstanding examples. These include:
—the National Writing Project in the U.S.A. in which teachers themselves exemplify the model;
—the official implementation of the model throughout the New Zealand education system through the work of the National English Syllabus Committee so that it is the norm.

iii. Since the Dartmouth Seminar of 1966 there has been much debate over the model and some misapprehension of it. It needs restating that:

—the model pays attention to both individual and social development, relating those carefully to one another. An emphasis upon individual growth is balanced by emphasis upon interaction with others as a means of such growth.

—the model is not therefore "romantic" in the sense of an over-emphasis upon the individual.

iv. The antithetical model is one which stresses:

—efficiency first, and

—order at the expense of individuality, freedom and personal or social growth.

v. We may have been guilty of underestimating the difficulties for teachers in implementing the model in terms of

—the constraints operating within schools as institutions, and

—the political realities in getting acceptance of the model.

We have been too squeamish about confronting the forces opposing us and somewhat naive in assessing their concerns and power.

2. The centrality of the teacher's position and role.

i. Work with teachers on the role of language in thinking and learning will make an enduring difference only when it seeks to change their beliefs as well as their practice.

ii. Teachers are more likely to accept the evidence from research when it accords with their beliefs.

iii. Teachers can benefit from constructing, each for herself, an explicit theory of knowledge and of discourse models and processes that flow from that theory.

iv. They need, therefore, to be involved in, and committed to, a re-theorizing of the teaching of their subject or grade.

v. Thus teachers will gain reflective control of their own knowledge and political control of the purposes and means of schooling.

vi. Rather than the creation of new courses in teacher training programmes, this is likely to mean the development of school-based projects involving collaborative relationships among teachers in schools as decision-makers, and desirably among schools, universities and curriculum centres.

vii. Educational administrators, decision-makers and the community need to be partners in the development of such school-based projects.

viii. Teachers are crucial to this process: the reality of the classroom is theirs; what they do determines what and how children learn.

They need to have more control over what affects them so directly. We affirm their right.

3. What teachers need.

    i. All teachers across the curriculum need to be enabled to reconceptualize the teaching/learning process.
    ii. Mere consciousness-raising is inadequate.
    iii. Mere exposure to recent theoretical concepts and developments will not ensure their practical application.
    iv. Comprehensive and dynamic projects are needed.

4. The politics of language and schooling.

The barriers to the implementation of language curricula designed to promote individual growth and effective social interaction are:

    i. Centralization and bureaucratization of educational decision making.
    ii. The extensive and indiscriminate use of insensitive testing.
    iii. Teacher education programmes that do not easily allow change in response to new theories and/or changing social needs.
    iv. The failure of scholars either to apply research findings or to translate them into language intelligible to teachers.
    v. Their failure, also, to communicate research findings effectively to policy makers and the testing profession.
    vi. Ignorance in the teaching profession about how educational decisions are made and how they might be influenced.

We must work to remove these barriers.

Recommendations for Action

In our study group entitled Language and Schooling were representatives of all five member countries of IFTE and a representative from Scotland as well. This mix achieved what were obviously the aims of the whole Seminar:

— It drew informed and caring educators together to exchange ideas and find areas of common concern about the state of English teaching today.
— It fostered our sense of urgency about the need for change in the education systems within which we all work.

The combination of these two factors is important because, as James Moffett said, it is belief and total commitment to a concept which will initiate in us the courage and determination to work for change. Our work as educationalists is the work of emancipationists, and often brings us into conflict with our governments. Hence our collective knowledge in the field of research and our joint experience in classroom practice must be turned into political action which will lead us to fight the pressures common in all our societies—those which devalue education, the arts, the humanities in general, and reduce the powers of the individual.

In making some recommendations for action, therefore, our study group sensed the potential power of our situation as an international body of educationalists and formulated the following demands for change:

1. The IFTE should form action committees to put pressure on governments and political parties to give education high priority in terms of money and aid, and to establish criteria by which the level of priority could be determined and judged.
2. The IFTE should advocate greater participation for classroom teachers along with politicians and administrators in designing curricula and in ongoing teacher training and inservice.
3. Teachers should be involved in active practical research and have more access to important research findings. Our members emphasised that teachers are more likely to work for change when they have gained a more reflective control of their own knowledge and a sense that their personal concerns have general relevance.
4. The IFTE should foster collaborative research in areas of common concern such as decision-making in our institutions, methods of assessment, standards of language competency, and the effects of failure on learners and teachers.
5. The success of the National Writing Project in the United States should be used as a model for establishing National Language Learning projects throughout our own countries. The significance of the model provided by the National Writing project includes:

   —extensive and extended inservice teacher training;
   —emphasis on a student-centred programme of learning; and
   —the use of a network structure to consolidate the work done.

And so to conclude—perhaps with a personal comment. What we have found so significant about the concerns expressed by our group, and therefore about its recommendations, is the twofold awareness of the factors that will operate to bring about change.

First, our collective strength has been recognised as a vital factor. This isn't the first time English teachers have met internationally but it is the first time we have met under the auspices of an organization of our own, the IFTE, which will be committed to follow up the process here begun.

Second, the classroom teacher must be an active participant in the move for change. She or he will not be able to work in isolation however. The process of change will need to be a collaborative one among administrators, politicians, community and teachers.

Conclusion and Summary

1. Impressions: Some significant successes recognised, some pain at not having been more successful; a feeling of being right, but not yet having carried the day; a sense of being embattled, of the strength of conservative forces; recognition of "academic drag" and political naiveté; commitment to press on, finding the ways and given the leadership—all these were part of the experience of the working group on Language and Schooling.
2. The personal growth model of language acquisition and the teacher were central to all that the group discussed and suggested.
3. The forces of conservatism ally all those who see control rather than empowerment as the end of education—many parents, politicians, administrators and teachers—those who, as James Moffett suggested, have a vested interest in "perpetuating the world that parents understand." Bureaucratic power structures depersonalize education, making it a matter of statistics. Teachers become practitioners rather than exponents.
4. Teachers of English need translators of theory and research into teacher practice to help them to make the commitment to reconceptualize their own teaching. We need solid evidence to present to those who doubt. We need those skilled in the politics of education to exert pressure where it will do most good, and to give our concerns a high public profile and a good press.
5. IFTE member associations and IFTE itself have important and complementary roles in meeting those needs: IFTE making representations, where appropriate, to international agencies and lending support to national associations; member associations working directly with teachers, government agencies and other national and regional bodies, and contributing to the richness of the exchange of ideas within IFTE.
6. IFTE members must recommit themselves to work and teach towards the use of language in schools as a liberating, enfranchising force, rather than a repressive, restrictive instrument.

Study Group 3:

Language and the New Media

Chair:
DAVID A. ENGLAND
Louisiana State University (U.S.A.)

The study group on "Language and the New Media" began by formulating questions and issues generally related to one of three broad fields which influence and are influenced by the media. As a result, one subgroup formed to discuss *media from a pedagogical perspective* and was primarily interested in the influence of media in and upon classroom instruction. A second subgroup considered *media from a socio-political perspective* and concerned itself with questions of media power and access. Our third subgroup considered *media and their effects from a psychological perspective*—how the media may be changing how we think, not just what we think, became the focus of that group's deliberations. We knew full well, of course, that such artificial distinctions as these were neither mutually exclusive nor sufficient.

The subgroup attending to pedagogical issues was most directly concerned with what has happened, is happening, and may happen as media, teachers, and kids get together in our classrooms. It offered the following observation:

> The history of the profession's relationship with new media has not always been productive. Sometimes teachers have embraced media with more enthusiasm than understanding of how such media should work within the English curriculum. Sometimes teachers have feared media and resisted using them or even learning how to use them. How to avoid these unproductive relationships with media is an important issue which must be addressed by teachers of English.

After having arrived at consensus on this point, members of this subgroup made the following recommendations:

The relationship of student and teacher with the mass media must be one which:

1. strengthens and furthers the "essentials" of teaching English in the spirit of the recent NCTE document, "The Essentials of Teaching English";
2. identifies and acts upon those barriers which impede media utilization;
3. helps students make informed critical and ethical decisions about media and the impact of media on their lives;
4. enables teachers and professional organizations to become actively involved in shaping, as well as using, the media that are part of the curriculum.

The following statements are representative of the issues defined and the recommendations made by the subgroup which discussed media from a socio-political perspective:

The greater our access to symbolization and the tools of language, literacy, and thinking, the greater our potential for making choices for life and for living. It is the depth of our potential for gaining access to information and to the ways of operating in the world, as well as for expressing ourselves, that empowers us as individuals.

Teachers have to understand that every use of media, like everything else which goes on in classrooms, carries with it a complex of values that informs learners about their station relative to knowledge and knowing. We need to see beyond the surface of software to the underlying values. We must weed out those uses of media which withhold control and initiative from learners, which limit rather than expand learners' views of learning and of knowledge.

English teachers will continue to value the literary traditions and conventional forms of expression. Students not only have a different set of expressive and artistic priorities; they often have a much wider experiential background with film, with television, and with computers. English teachers must explore the connections between the culture and experiences which *they* value and the culture and experiences which their students value.

The power relationships in which students participate in classrooms may model, predict, and/or determine the power relationships in which they participate as members of the larger society. It is imperative that students interact emotionally and intellectually with teachers, peers, and media in ways designed to empower them with a sense of worth, value, and the ability to participate in the broader society.

In spite of the ubiquity of the electronic media in today's world, success in school is still largely a language matter. The media are potential tools for improving and expanding language learning in the classroom, but the potential is largely ignored by the English teaching profession. Even if all children in our society *did have* adequate access to computer word processing (and there is the possibility that many never will) English teachers would still have to determine whether the use of word processing at particular grade levels would be beneficial or detrimental, what specific uses of word processing would be appropriate, and how much word processing would be desirable. Language learning would still be central; so too, would judgment by the teacher. If one adds the prospects for media "haves and have-nots" to the issue, the whole problem becomes quite complex.

Summary: The new media have the potential to enrich students' understanding of, engagement with, and participation in the symbol-making systems of their world. It is essential that educators use collaborative projects in which media are central to collapse the traditional classroom hierarchies (i.e., teacher-student; student-student in individual competition) and to promote a greater equality in how power is distributed. The following two assumptions are implicit in the above points, and each is likely to prove controversially problematic. First, the new media have a potentially enriching capacity and therefore argue for a legitimate role in the language curriculum. Secondly, the traditional structure and balances of power in the classroom inhibit learning and should therefore be replaced by more equal distribution of power among teachers and learners.

The third subgroup considered how media may be changing how we think and the psychologies of the children we teach. Its statement:

Ironically, the central issue arising from the confrontation between English and media other than print as they impinge on the psychological processes of students may have little to do with the nature of the teaching/learning environment of the English classroom. That is, some of the answers to questions surrounding the study and teaching of various media in the classroom will be found only insofar as we examine the roles these media play in the lives of our students and the understandings and misunderstandings both we and our students share as a result of and through these various media. And so we begin properly with a story.

In a discussion with a group of secondary school students, we asked which television shows they liked most and why they enjoyed these particular shows. Although favorites varied considerably, almost immediately one group of students closed forces around *Hill Street Blues* while another began to defend *General Hospital*. Both groups explained their choices by affirming the *reality* of those shows: *Hill Street* showed what police work was really like, and *General Hospital* presented real people with real problems. As we collectively began to examine what "real" meant in this discussion, the students came to agree that neither show was, in their terms, "really real"; that, in fact, a presentation of and/or an examination of reality had little or nothing to do with their viewing preferences. In the ensuing confusion and frustration, it became increasingly clear that both students and teacher were not only unsure of our reasons for watching certain shows, but we also lacked a vocabulary, a way of articulating our reasons. This discussion revealed once again the need to center on the students' experiences as learners, and on their private and collective explorations of these experiences in order to assist them in understanding better themselves, others, and their ways of being in the world.

For us, the point of this story is simple: the insistent presence of the media—their importance in both our own and our students' lives—exposes once again all of our basic assumptions about the role of the teacher in convening learning encounters in the classroom. At the same time it raises a serious question: Is media to be viewed as yet another burden of content for the teacher to cover or transmit, or, like the composing and reading processes, as an opportunity for exploring, critiquing, and extending the theories of reality in the world that the students bring with them? In this regard, the wisdom of the 1966 Dartmouth conference serves us well: though never forgetting the importance of certain basic skills and the richness of our cultural heritage, we can never lose sight of the importance of the individual student's personal growth. Such a conception of English, we must remember, never gave license for isolated, egocentric self-expression; rather, it allowed teachers to create a curriculum that engaged and legitimized student experience in order that their constructs of this experience, embedded as they were in the interpersonal context of community, would develop and mature in depth and intensity leading to a sense of common humanity.

While this model of English represents an ideal, it is important to remember that its wide dissemination remains but a vague hope, an unrealized potential. It's our contention, however, that the continuing challenge of all media is that they can serve as powerful incentives for us to keep reexamining the priorities and assumptions of our profession. From this perspective we suggest that the following questions guide our inquiry and practices as teachers of English: 1) How do the media change and/or determine the way our students construct reality? 2) What is the effect of these changes, if any, on the ways students come to approach traditional literacy tasks? 3) How might we better go about understanding and appreciating these new constructs and realities of our students?

Recommendations: First, though we don't suggest or even encourage that all English teachers become "media experts," we do stress the need for all English teachers to share in some way in the media experiences of their students by having firsthand knowledge of the media themselves. Teachers should use word processing, employ videotape for recording live and televised events, use film, take photographs, and even occasionally listen to popular contemporary music; for it is only through this direct and personal experience with the media that we can begin to understand how they affect and influence meaning-making processes (orally, through print, and through other media). Furthermore, such direct experience with media is the only way for teachers to share in this aspect of the common culture. We believe that young people growing up in a media-rich culture, foreign to our own pre-computer developmental experience, are inalterably different language learners. We need to find ways of bridging this fundamental generation gap by trying to glimpse, if but through a glass darkly, our students' ways of experiencing and constructing reality.

Secondly, as teachers, we need to engage actively in researching, from an ethnographic perspective, the meanings our students are experiencing as they transact with the new media. The following example, though taken from a writing class, suggests an approach applicable to all English teachers. After sensing that her students in a lower-level writing program appeared to be responding differently when writing by hand than when composing on the computer, the teacher went on to frame a number of questions: How does the word processor affect the writer's relationship to his or her text? How do students deal with their fears of the computer failing and the text becoming lost? How do varying word processing programs change the procedures students use in composing? How does the size of the video screen and thus the amount of text it can display at any one time alter the way students hold on to and manipulate units of thought? How does the fluidity of the screen affect the revision process? How does this writing technology change students' approaches to error correction and detection? With these questions in mind, the teacher began more actively observing the behavior patterns of her students and directly tapping their insights and attitudes. She noticed, for instance, that despite her frequent coaching to "Keep going. Don't worry about writing complete sentences," many students kept sneaking the cursor back to insure that capitals and periods were all neatly in place. As she probed further, she began to realize how deeply engrained the idea of correctness was in the reward system the students had been previously taught and had evidently retained. She thus tried modifying the word processing program in two ways: she cut the amount of text that appeared in any one instant down to two lines, and further, she built in a "trap" that prevented students from moving the cursor backward without her permission. Her students complained at first, but became more comfortable with a more fluid composing process. By continuing to ask questions and probe the computer environment as it was being interpreted by her students, this teacher was doing on-the-spot research which, in turn, was immediately informing her teaching strategies. Our charge, then, is for all of us as teachers to assume such a stance so that ongoing inquiry plays a vital role in the script we enact in our classrooms.

  Conclusion: English teachers must be encouraged, supported, and even directly trained in media literacy. They must learn to view literature (both print and non-print) as a representation of the human condition open to private and public interpretation which leads to the personal/social growth of the individual. They must come to respect their students' delight in various electronic media and commit themselves to exploring in the classroom the *students.* world of media. This exploration must be devoid of preaching ("See why you shouldn't watch soaps!") and innoculation ("What is the theme of this episode of *All in the Family*?") As was suggested at Dartmouth in 1966, the students' experience with the media must be central; various means should be made available for the students to share these experiences (orally, in writing, through art, etc.); and this sharing should become the basis for the collective negotiations of *reality* as well as the cornerstone for each individual's continuing act of self creation in the midst of their selves. Indeed, 1984 is hardly the time to reject the Dartmouth conference, but rather it is the time to reassert its central principles and continue exploring both the theoretical and the practical implications of focusing on the students' personal growth in an increasingly impersonal world.

A few points remain to be made about the spirit and experiences and perceptions of those who were members of the "media group."

First, we convened as teachers and professors, and we operated in our study group as learners. We realized that to learn isn't always to produce a finished product and that a product is never really finished nor fully reflective of what has been learned and shared. Our learning in the media group was at times messy and uneven, but it was often marvelous. It didn't lead easily to broad generalizations, and it certainly didn't encourage us to pontificate about what others "ought to be doing." We have thus approached this final report tentatively, viewing it as a work in progress.

Secondly, by the end of the conference, we realized how much we had taken for granted in assuming that other educators, let alone "the public," shared our notion that the media are worthy of educators' attention. To those of us who are interested in the media, it was only natural to assume that all people are similarly interested in media and media education. But then we realized that those in the study group on literature suffered under somewhat the same delusion regarding *their* special interest. We left believing that if the problems of assumed importance in the rest of the world were alike in kind, they were nonetheless different in degree. We were, after all, considering "new" media. And we understood that regardless of how central language may be to whatever is done with or by those "new" media, their study still does not, for many, have much to do with English.

Thirdly, we left with a rather skittish irony on the periphery of our attention: during the time we worked together, we did not, in the media subgroup, make any use whatsoever of any media. (In fact, the photocopy machine, which might have proven an exception, wasn't working on the day this subtle irony was finally articulated.) This point is by no means to be a reflection on the conference organizers or hosts—their planning and services were excellent. Rather, for all our talk of media, and despite the great convenience that, say, a word processor might have been as we did some group composing,

we made do with chalk and a chalk board—and white chalk only, as
Tony Adams wryly observed. That the media are "here and among
us" seems inarguable. When it comes to education, however, that
"here" and "us" needs careful definition and consideration.

Finally, we knew we were "different" among this assemblage
of English educators. If "lunatic fringe" suggests too much of the
way we felt (and have felt before at other conferences), then "different" perhaps suggests too little. We have less research. We have less
theory. We have fewer seminal works to reflect upon and to draw
from. We were, and still are, in a sense, much more inclined to evolve
tentative formulations and to ask questions. The "answers" to media
"problems" have too often only been retranslations of approaches
that worked in print-dominated culture. Such solutions are too
quickly obsolete, if they were every really applicable.

But then, who would have thought that a clever teenager with
the proper computer accessing skills could be a threat to a giant cor-
poration, or to national security? And who, twenty-five years ago,
really believed that as many as one hundred television signals could
reach our homes? Or that third graders would be using word proces-
sors? But here we are. (Or should that be, there we were?)

In the midst of all the fluidity and change and evolution on the
heels of evolution, there are those "media types" who are convened
at more and more conferences, and who, increasingly, have conferences of their own. Some are integrated (the media with each other,
or in the "language arts") while others are more segregated (computers *only* conferences). That the earliest planning of this IFTE
Conference allowed a major strand to be devoted to the media was,
to many of us, a fact noteworthy and not to be taken for granted.
We will, all of us media types, look forward to a day when the centrality of media in our convenings is not noteworthy and is, in fact,
a consideration one would take for granted.

Some "Process Reflections" by Members of the Media Study Group

At the end of each working session, members of the media
study group were asked to jot down a few reflections on where they
or their groups were, or where they were heading, or just what was
going on, at the moment, in their minds as they thought back over
what had been transpiring in their groups. What follows are some
"context free" comments drawn from these in-process formulations:

When computers arrive at a school, teachers should ask *first*
How can I use them to further literacy, *not* How can we adjust

our curriculum to make some of our students "computer literate."

(Richard Gebhardt, U.S.A.)

We still need to go back to a personal growth model (one that is socially contextualized) and not be seduced into thinking our responsibility involves merely teaching the "grammar" of the new media or revealing facts about its history, economics, etc.

(Gordon Pradl, U.S.A.)

A major remaining issue is the place of TV, video, rock video, and related media forms and capabilities. This seems to me to be a much more immediate issue for the kinds of culture and ideology which prevail in any community today . . .

(John Collerson, Australia)

How do the power relationships between teachers and students change when students know more about TV, video and computers than the teacher?

(Claire Woods, Australia)

All teachers are busy and must be given time to think about and process what they are doing and will be asked to do with media; whether through in-service or just planning time, teachers need time to think and to reflect.

(Diana Mitchell, U.S.A.)

The media will not destroy Shakespeare, but will create new kinds of Shakespeare and ways of knowing Shakespeare and ways of doing Shakespeare in the future.

(Ron Santora, U.S.A.)

Many questions and overwhelming considerations arose this past hour and a half—plus, long periods of silence . . . that awful, dreaded, "Somebody please say *something*" silence. We needed this time, yet the beginnings are not always enjoyable when we toss around something none of us are quite clear about.

(Nancy Johnson, U.S.A.)

Study Group 4:

Language, Literature, and Human Values

Chair:
GARTH BOOMER
Curriculum Development Centre,
Canberra (Australia)

Prior to the IFTE Seminar, Garth Boomer prepared a charge to the thirty people who made up this study group. At the same time, eleven of the participants-to-be were writing brief working papers, and the consultant, Louise Rosenblatt, also provided notes related to her address, which appears elsewhere in this book.

The working papers covered a very wide territory. (For a full listing of study group papers, see Appendix B.) Deanne Bogdan (Canada) opened up an issue which remained a priority throughout the seminar: depicting literary response as a dialectic she argued that literary knowledge is a "legitimate component of literary experience." She advocated that we enjoy the best of both worlds, engagement and detachment.

David Dillon (Canada) explored the relationship between *literacy* and *literature.* Using personal construct theory he boldly depicted literature as a key element in the shaping of the person: "Encountering literature is like meeting another person (or persons) who reveal themselves honestly and completely." Literature is like a mirror into which the reader looks for material which will help in his or her continuing construction of the self.

Ken Macrorie (U.S.A.) anticipated one of the key issues later to be identified by the group as crucial to the teaching of literature—the professional development of teacher educators in the field of literature so that teachers engage dynamically with literature:

"In the universities, which directly and indirectly shape education, we are so committed to ancient caste notions that few of us have ever stepped outside the established demarcation lines. But when we do, we find that studying and writing with learners whose culture we respect is far more exciting and enjoyable than just handing down the word from above."

Wendy Sutton (Canada) showed how alternative modes of writing fiction are extending the "vast range of thought and experience which literature permits to co-exist."

By preference to her own experience as a parent of children who are developing relationships with literature, Susan Tchudi (U.S.A.) showed how her own values interact with the emerging value systems of her children. A continuing tension between respect for the individual (often seen as a Dartmouth concern) and the significance of group collaboration was felt not only in the literature strand but in the seminar as a whole. Tchudi, while acknowledging the power of interaction, recognized "the complexity and integrity of the individual."

Reporting on research in both Canada and England on patterns of student response to literature, Patrick Dias (Canada) identified four different stances which students take. His research, linked to the work of Rosenblatt, suggests that some students learn to be efferent readers. The problem-solving reader seems able to reconcile both *efferent* and *aesthetic* responses.

On the same theme, Nancy Lester (U.S.A.) took up Rosenblatt's notions of efferent and aesthetic readings and suggested that we have a strong obligation as teachers of literature to help students understand the power of adopting an aesthetic stance toward a literary text.

Richard Corballis (New Zealand) provided a provocative, divergent view on the same issue. As a drama teacher he plays the iconoclast to Leavis's notions of reading as a "collaborative-creative process," treating the text instead as a decipherable self-consistent world which makes logic the central strategy of reading.

Possibly mediating between Lester and Corballis, W. John Harker (Canada) extended some of the ideas seeded by Bogdan and offered some antidotes to the view that readers construct the work. He acknowledged that reading is an individual "event" that happens as each reader interacts with the text, but he also argued that literature conveys its own meaning, a special knowledge about literature itself. He concluded that:

"An awareness and a sensitivity to the terminology of literature can be taught by actively demonstrating how literature "works" by showing how configurations of conventions and features which literature displays, shape its meaning and even its intent in the minds of readers."

John Oster (Canada) and James Davis (U.S.A.) enriched our understanding of what it might be to be a good teacher of literature.

Both advocated radical changes to the traditional view of literature teaching. Oster depicted good teaching of literature as a muscular, active participation of teacher and student in the "sport" of reading and writing and Davis reminded us that what we teach is the way we teach. He will obviously try to teach in a way that shows how he continually reflects on himself as an emerging "text." "Watch how I make and re-make myself in the light of my reflections."

Beginning Questions and Issues

In the opening meeting of the study group, participants in this strand each reflected on the issues raised in the working papers and Boomer's challenge and wrote a brief piece setting down the *one* issue that ought to be explored above all others. These early writings were collated into a list which was circulated and which represented a multi-directional signpost indicating where people might go. The next task was to simplify all this into four or five broad directions so that sub-groups could form and begin to work.

Questions and Issues

1. How has literature, broadly defined, been used in schools in the past to empower students and how can it be used in the future to empower even more? And conversely, how has literature been used in schools to control, blinker, diminish and distort human valuing and human intention?
2. What are the inconsistencies between the act of "teaching" literature and the nature of the transaction that occurs between a reader and a literary text?
3. In what ways can the teaching of literature (i.e. writing and reading as aesthetic transactions) contribute to helping children develop the ability to think constructively about problems of values?
4. What is the nature of the relationship of the individual and the cultural group with respect to the reading of literature?
5. Will emphasis on collective experience lead to regression in teaching (i.e. less individual processing of diverse texts)?
6. Will pressures for "quality" literature work against perceptions of student writing as literature?
7. How can we effect connections between "given" literature and the stories that students can/must tell?
8. The most pressing question relates to the matter of *intentions*. *Thesis:* that children's pre-occupations and concerns give the directions which shape their responses to the books they *choose*

to read and also the things they *choose* to write about.
So: we need to consider the place of student intentions in reading and writing.

9. We need to do something about students' frequent complaint that the literature that belongs to the teacher is boring.
10. Do values proceed from literature to reader or *vice versa* from reader to literature? And if from literature to reader, do the values come explicitly via the content or implicitly via the style/form. Or both?
11. We need to explore the role or function of the teacher in developing students' relationships with literature and in particular the relationships between writing and reading in developing engagement with literature.
12. Why read literature? What claims can we make for its value to the lives of our students in justifying it in the curriculum? What makes literature work for people?
13. How do we help children to have intentions to read literature?
14. We need to address the increasing emphasis on screen reading and writing.
15. What can we claim for the centrality of the arts in education?
16. Literature reflects personal, anthropological or cultural values. Does adult or juvenile literature express values which are destructive or creative for society and individuals?
17. The English teacher is an adult, a person trained in a way that has resulted in a very specialized set of values, tastes, attitudes towards language and literature. The students' attitudes, tastes, etc. are probably less formed, more typically human and quite different from the teacher's. How can we bring about a communion between teacher and student so that literature can work for both?
18. Can we arrive at consensus concerning selection of literature without suggesting a prescribed and fixed canon? Are there some books or themes or topics that are more fruitful for group exploration at various ages and stages? Why do we select certain books? Do we make clear why?
19. We need to look at literary/poetic discourse in a larger context of society/culture than we have. We need to see it as a reflection and cause of organic, dynamic cultures in society. What is *the reason* for literature? And how does this all fit with the context of classrooms?
20. We need to find a better alternative to the "response" metaphor.
21. How can we best engage students in texts (their own or others) so that students care; care enough to form values, change values, refine values?

22. We need to explore ways of moving from the initial personal response to the more analytical assessment of literature and an examination of language used.

23. How does one reconcile the apparent difference in classrooms where personal response is valued and encouraged with the "measures" and expected "outcomes" often imposed by outside agencies?

24. How can the use of language help the individual reconstrue (in George Kelly's terms) who he/she is?

25. We need to learn how to mediate between an "experience" perspective on the reading of literature (as opposed to, say a formalist perspective) and the fact that our interests as teachers include concern for literature in forms and from time periods that makes it less than immediately accessible to our students.

26. We need to reject the organic form model of literature, including its formulation by Britton as "poetic" discourse.

27. We need to clarify and explore the ways in which values (moral, social, personal, literary, aesthetic) *enter* a literary work and how teachers can help students deal with their processing of these multifarious kinds of value through language.

28. We need to address the context of learning in schools, the value systems of schools and how this context and the value systems may clash with that of students, especially in the way language is used, or expected to be used (e.g. the student who learns mainly by watching and possibly talking.)

29. How do we deal with indoctrination when clearly as teachers we have value systems ourselves and a role to play in shaping values?

30. It has been said that secondary teachers know how to teach a book, elementary teachers how to teach a child. How might the balance of experiencing/sharing with analysing change across the years of schooling?

31. How should literature be learned in school? What kinds of learning do teachers need to have in order to be able to teach in a way other than through "lit. crit."?

32. Should there be any concern about whose (or what) values are being illuminated? Is it possible to ignore "human values"? If it is not, how do value considerations get introduced, dealt with, joined, illuminated?

33. What do we know about what "literature sense" students of all ages bring to school?

34. How can our view of ourselves, others, the world, be changed reverberatingly as a result of the literature we read?

35. How does the response of others affect our response?
36. What is it that children "learn to do" when they learn to "read" literature? What is it about literature that must be learned as opposed to what the reader brings to literature?
37. How do readers make meaning out of literature? How do they create the reality in which they live (values, attitudes, beliefs, expectations) during their transaction with literary works?

Group Work

Working from the initial list of questions and issues the strand eventually formed four sub-groups to deal with the following issues:

1. Reading and writing in the early years as a shaper of constructs about literature.
2. The education of teachers for better teaching and learning of literature.
3. Intention, indoctrination and human values in symbol making and story telling.
4. What makes and stops the working of literature?

The first group grappled with questions about how young children make meaning and how teachers may provide effective *contexts* for learning in schools. The following excerpt from their notes indicates some of their concerns:

> We do not know if there is a developmental progression in reader response or if the text itself, style of discourse, length, register, pictures, etc. have a discernible influence on reader response. Nor do we know how in developing literacy, classroom activities influence reader response. We need to explore these issues, as well as the ways classroom response activities enhance the kinds of meaning children bring to a text. One area of response which deserves special attention is the connection between reading and children's own writing of literature. If children respond to a selected text in writing, how does the experience enhance comprehension and/or writing? In the Dartmouth tradition we want children to take control of their own learning and make meaning in many situations and with many kinds of texts. Approaches to achieve this goal should be studied.

One member of this group, David Dillon, wrote these reflections on several areas of discussion:

My major concern still centers on "What's literature for?" or "Why use it to foster response to it?"—whatever that is. The group is struggling to deal with it. I think we must constantly keep our eye on where the literacy experience takes us, its "effect" on us, what it's for—whether that be human growth, the making of culture, emotional release, other outcomes, or all of the above. I don't want us to fall into teaching literary response as a *process*—as if it were devoid of social, cultural, and political context. An important part of this is viewing literature as a particular way of knowing (cognitive yes, but also emotional, experiential, intuitive). In this sense, literature begins to make sense not so much as a separate subject area, but rather as literature across the curriculum. It also prompts me to think again of an alternative to the "response" metaphor.

Another major area of concern of mine focuses on the early years of schooling (at least most of the elementary grades in North America). In such a secondary dominated group, I hope that we can make a special contribution. An elementary focus is important in several ways:

a. There has been relatively little use of literature in the elementary years and probably a somewhat different kind of use than in secondary years. I think it helpful if we view the teaching of literature as at least a common enterprise all through school and perhaps as somewhat developmental (although I'm not happy with that term). Jimmy Britton gives us a little bit of help with the developmental aspects of his discourse model (i.e. growth from an expressive core toward poetic discourse in one direction), but generally we know almost nothing about the literary experiences of young children up to 9 years of age and precious little about the 10–12 years range (where the usual "response" research starts). This reminds me too that we know little, I think, about the "culture" of childhood, what their worlds, constructs, and values are—which will determine their experience with literature as well as be shaped by it. I'd like to see a research focus on the development and growth of early literary experiences just as concentrated and exciting as the research on, first, oral language development and, later, on early literacy.

b. A second issue in elementary schools is the teaching of reading and writing which most of us seem to agree is rather counterproductive to literary experiences. The separation of literacy and literature seems to be a key concern as is the efferent model of reading and writing most literacy instruction is based on. It seems we need to redefine literacy in such a way as to link it more with literature. The challenge for elementary teachers is to not teach reading and writing primarily (for that can make them ends in themselves and separate them from the what and why of language use), but to teach literature (life?) primarily with reading and writing developing as concomitants.

The group looking at the question of teacher education was particularly concerned with identifying features of a good classroom (particularly at the university level, for the teaching of literature). A good deal of discussion centred on the tension for the teacher between individual and group work. The dimensions of the question are explored by Jim Davis in some private writing:

Independence as an individual participating in a society is one basic I value in my human condition. I am empowered with that independence through my ability to *reflect*, to examine my own life and the lives of others, in part through oral and written literature. Paradoxically, owning and perpetuating my *in*dependence *depends* on interaction with others—others from whom to be independent, but also with whom, through whom to clarify, extend, refine my transactions with texts. My individual good is served neither if I deny my collective responsibilities *nor* if I give myself over completely to them. If I believe this situation to be true of others, then as a teacher I face the tension, potentially productive, of attending simultaneously to the individual and to the group—i.e. accepting obligation to the individual and the collective good. I do not accept that the collective good is served in the abrogation of the individual, nor that the individual good is served through ignoring the collective context. What I value for both is informed reflection—as individuals must examine their lives, actions, beliefs, so too must societies, the classroom society, the school, the community and beyond. Ultimately, the ability and inclination to so reflect is inculcated through modelling and experience, both of which can be accomplished in part in the classroom. I believe the profession should affirm, as an assumed, fundamental cultural value, that the *examined* life is worth living and the continually examined society may allow living to continue. Our consciousness of collective existence, even the global collective, will not serve society well if we fail to maintain the visibility of the individual. And as yet, that post-Dartmouth visibility has only shallowly penetrated the collective consciousness of our profession.

The third group looked closely at the social, institutional and political context of literature teaching. Participants identified constraints on teaching such as large class sizes and inadequate preparation of teachers of literature. They did not place blame on teachers for teaching in ways which cut across student intentions and they recognized fully the kind of support, from administrators, especially, which teachers at all levels will need in order to change to a different role as partners and enablers.

The final statement of the whole group includes a section on imperatives that relate to contexts for literature teaching. Much of this section was contributed by the third group.

The final group worked closely with Louise Rosenblatt to explore the working of literature transactions between readers and texts. After reaching a definition of literature they teased out pedagogical implications and related these implications to questions of values and valuing.

Notes from a strand member, Pat D'Arcy, indicate some of the issues relating to the question of good teaching.

> Perhaps we should address ourselves to the point about teachers as specially experienced and reflective readers who can comment upon the reading process. We need to spell out more specifically what that implies for the role and functions of the teacher of literature at the primary, secondary and tertiary phases. For instance, does it mean knowing as an experienced reader of literature, what to offer next to individual 8-year-olds or 11-year-olds, from an on-the-ground knowledge of what they are currently reading? Does it mean being able to ask open rather than closed questions that will challenge individual readers to think more deeply? Does it mean knowing how to encourage children to shape their *own* stories/poems/plays and thereby develop fresh insights into how others have done this?

From the working papers, the challenge, the deliberations of the small groups, grew a consensus (though by no means unanimous) of the central issues and priorities in language, literature, and human values. In the interests of seeing ideas reach as many different people, the members of the study group prepared:

A Statement:

On Language, Literature, and Human Values

(Addressed to councils and associations of member countries of IFTE, education authorities and agencies, teacher educators and teachers at all levels)

Introduction

What follows is one result of the deliberations of the strand on *Language, Literature, and Human Values*. It represents only a small part of a complex and multi-faceted seminar. Participants were aware of the need to make available to their colleagues around the world, the outcomes of their deliberations but they wished to do this, not in the manner of delivery from the summit, but rather as a considered contribution to the conversations and projects which must continue long after East Lansing. They were specially conscious of the small number of elementary and secondary teachers present and indicated that IFTE in future meetings of this kind should devise ways os supporting teacher attendance.

This section is written so that it might stand alone as a discussion paper to inform policy making groups in systems, schools, universities, colleges, and other educational agencies or as a reference point for groups of teachers and parents engaged in debates about the teaching of literature.

Definition

Literature is any text, verbal and/or visual, that offers the possibility for aesthetic reading or viewing and listening. The literariness resides in the transaction between reader and text or viewer and performance. A literary work comes into being when there is a transaction between text and reader in which personal experience with the work is primary. Such reading provides pleasure and contributes to a shared culture. The making and reading of literature is a fundamental and essential human activity.

The Purposes of Literature Teaching

Interpretation during and following the experience of making and reading literature can enable children *to become more self aware; more sensitive to both the uniqueness of the individual and the shared culture;* and *more knowledgeable about the ongoing cultural dialogue directed towards great issues which shape people and which they in turn shape.* The reading, writing and discussing of literature in schools should aim at enhanced ability to *reflect,* to take stances and act accordingly, through encounters with diverse texts and with other readers and writers.

Imperatives in Relation to the Contexts of Literature Teaching

• Teachers need to help students to make a commitment to their education. Mutual effort will, in this way, make room for mutual intentions.

• Children bring life experiences into their classrooms (competences, expectations, values and cultural differences). These are paramount and teachers must learn them, build on them and negotiate the curriculum from them.

• *Teacher educators* must tackle the change to a different role for teachers. Teachers will need a great deal of help and support, if they are expected to become partners and enablers, constantly planning in the light of developing negotiations in the classroom.

• Administrators must support teachers who are trying to change their role.

Fundamental Principles

• Storytelling is an important way of making sense of experience.

• Children should be involved in both *the reading* and *the writing* of literature.

• Literary exploration should involve the child in making literature as well as reading it.

• Readers and writers must become involved in the continuing efforts of society to forge meaning out of experience by investigating *a wide range of literary texts, their own, those of other cultures* and *those from other times.*

• The unique perspective of the individual and thus the unique meaning made by each reader and writer must be respected.

• There are multiple defensible interpretations of any text.

• Any act of reading and writing should address itself first to meanings (the meaning that the reader brings to the text as well as the meanings that the writer brought to it) and over a period of time to how these meanings intermingle and create fresh perspectives for the reader.

• The goal of literature teaching is the enfranchisement and empowerment of children as learners and actors in the making of culture.

• The ability to handle texts evolves through talking and sharing of elaborated responses to texts both made and read.

• Children's writing contributes to the range of world literatures by representing children's views of the world at an important developmental stage of their lives.

Implications for the Teaching of Literature

• The "literature" class by the tenets presented above would be a community supportive of the making of meaning and the exploration of meaning in and through literary texts.

• Both teachers and children need to articulate their interpretations of literature (their own writing and that of other authors) so that these can be

a. shared
b. tracked for changes over time and through continued sharing.

• The teacher is one reader among many. The teacher is one interpreter of the text but a specially experienced and reflective reader who can comment on the reading process and share many ways of exploring the meanings that emerge.

• A major drive of classroom discussion of literature will be towards *sustained reflection* on issues or choice in values so that children generate the drive to *act* on their understandings of what is worthy and desirable. This means enhanced awareness of where they stand on value questions, and where there are tensions between their values and the values of others.

• The literary transaction in schools will involve

a. sympathetic identification
b. discovery and affirmation of values and attitudes
c. questioning of values and attitudes
d. movement towards new values and attitudes
e. increased ability to understand self and others.

(N.B. None of these need cut across delight in how language can shape thought and feeling.)

• Ideally the reading and making of literature will satisfy arousal and result in fulfilment in terms of feeling, thought, memory and understanding.

• Classrooms *for* literature teaching will be places of continuing and varied face-to-face exchanges, teacher to student, student to student, student to group and therefore (for organizational and educational reasons) classes will need to be smaller than has been customary to date.

• Teachers working to these principles might teach a literature program with the following goals:

a. To cause personal transactions between the student and the text rather than emphasizing the text alone.
b. To promote students' sharing their personal responses, understandings and meanings with other students as well as the teacher to create a dialogue which enables the individual to refine, deepen, or reshape his/her connections with the literature. This means that within a community of learners, this sharing may take many forms: telling, questioning, responding, comparing, contrasting on a one to one basis, in small groups, and in large groups. Students should be free to select the form of response best suited to their needs and interests at any given time.
c. To provide opportunities for student self-selection of literature.
d. To promote the development of self-motivated discerning readers.
e. To provide opportunities for the production of literature as well as the reading of it so that students will become more sophisticated readers and writers.
f. To help students discover that the uniqueness of literature comes from the ability of the reader to connect the literature read with his or her experience.

• The preparation of teachers to work in such a program might include the following:

a. Successful experiences of their own as readers and writers of literature.
b. Practical application in implementing the process.
c. Understanding of the theory behind the process.
d. Development of the skills necessary to work with students to select transactions that in many cases also will permit meaningful and pleasurable transactions about literature with other students.

Key Issues

Empowerment

We need to document how literature, broadly defined, has been used in schools in the past to empower students to gain greater influence over decisions which affect them, to act independently on their own behalf, and to understand "the ways of the world" and how it can be used in the future to empower even more. And conversely we need also to document how literature has been and is used in schools to control, blinker, diminish and distort human valuing and human intention.

Intentions

The most pressing question in relation to empowerment relates to *intentions*. We believe that children's pre-occupations and concerns give the direction which shape their responses to the books they *choose* to read and also the things they *choose* to write about. A major challenge to teachers at all levels is to develop teaching practices which allow for, take account of, and mobilise student intentions in reading and writing.

Teaching

We need to explore the role or function of the teacher of literature. New understandings of literary transactions call for better theories for the teaching of literature. These, in turn, will have implications *for the education of teachers of literature*. University and tertiary teachers of our teachers in elementary and secondary schools will need to behave congruently with the theories (and practices) which they espouse. In elementary/primary and secondary schools teachers will need to investigate new ways of observing children's reading and writing so that they can provide better learning contexts based on what they know about the learners. The implications for new methods of teaching are profound and complex. Strong support will be needed for teacher investigations.

Explicitness

In order to teach learners how to become better readers and writers of literature, teachers need to practise it, demonstrate it and comment explicitly on how they do it themselves. This requires the ability to articulate the theories which drive their practice and furthermore the *desire* and the *capacity* to make these theories available to learners.

Just as in learning the acts of reading and writing, demonstrations and running commentary on demonstrations are potent, so in the making, reading and interpreting of literature, engagement with how others behave and think in the literary act, will powerfully influence learners.

Literature

The word "literature" carries connotations of a fixed and homogeneous body of texts and adhering to this are notions of a fixed and worthy canon of works. (Usually in our schools ethnocentric and culturally exclusive.) Just as it is simplistic to think of "literacy" so it is limiting to think of "literature." These is a need to recognize the full range of literatures wherever these are made and read.

Response

We need to achieve a better understanding of the notion of reader "response." Response theory does not stop with mere response. Unexplored, the word "response" may too readily suggest reaction to a text almost on a stimulus-response model. This tends to distract us from a full apprehension of how literature is socially and ideologically constructed in the first place and then re-made in the act of reading. It also tends to lead to a pedagogy where mere *response* is validated. We need to consider the personal and societal uses of literature as a form of discourse. We need to develop constructive social criticism in going beyond response *to consider action*.

Indoctrination

The question of *whose values* are being considered in classrooms *in whose interests* is a matter of vital concern to us. It is acknowledged that teachers cannot and should not avoid the powerful presentation of their own values. Open revelation and discussion by teachers of their own values in such a way that they are subject to critique and are not imposed seems to be the most honest and constructive approach to the matter of values. There is a need to clarify and explore the ways in which values enter a work of literature and how these can be identified and processed by teachers and students to promote critical cultural literacy (the ability to read and write one's world) rather than glib acceptance or rejection. The question of values and indoctrination is complicated by the fact that classroom acts take place in institutions which carry value systems which are often militant against the values of individuals and groups of students.

The Individual and the Group

We acknowledge that initially the act of reading is private but we also know that what is learnt privately can be extended through more public (i.e. one to one, small group, whole class, etc.) sharing and critical reflection on what has been learnt. The art of teaching is to recognize and allow for the private and tacit dimensions of reading and writing as well as public sharing and scrutiny of opinions and ideas.

Recommendations

1. That where possible, the councils and associations of member countries of IFTE take up the issues identified in this statement and discuss them at teacher meetings and conferences.

2. That education systems, universities, and other agencies promote action-oriented projects to investigate, document and share findings addressing issues identified in this statement.

3. That all bodies and agencies involved in the teaching of literature but particularly councils and associations for the teaching of English and reading, specifically address the development of more powerful and useful theories for the teaching of literature through the establishment of working parties and networks both within and across countries.

4. That education systems, teacher education institutions and in-service agencies, consider the mounting of teacher development projects with respect to literature teaching/reading, based on principles which promote and support communities of teachers as practitioners, researchers and critical reflectors on their own classroom actions.

   (N.B. Such projects in the realm of writing have been mounted successfully in all member countries of IFTE over the past five years.)

5. That specifically such projects focus on capturing in ethnographic detail the *contexts* for reading offered to children in the course of a school day, week, term, year; the *reading behaviour* of children and the *outcomes* of reading.

6. That such projects also document what happens when students share with teachers in mapping the expanding terrain of their own response to and interpretation of books.

7. That since basal readers promote wrong and distorted constructions about literature and since they are not literature but artificial con-

structs for the teaching of reading, associations, councils, teacher groups and parents should take action to have them removed from schools.

8. That curriculum agencies, teacher educators, school boards, teachers and appropriate teacher associations should oppose the separation of instruction for literacy from "literature" teaching in the elementary/primary school curriculum.

9. That studies be mounted in universities, systems and schools, to document how response to literature through drama, movement, the visual arts and creative writing can enhance interpretation and learning.

Study Group 5:
Language and
Multicultural Education

Chair:
YETTA GOODMAN
University of Arizona (U.S.A.)

The members of the International Federation for the Teaching of English who participated in the study group on language and multicultural education included representatives from all levels of professional education with expertise in such areas as the *study of literature, applied linguistics, reading, composition, language arts, multilingualism, school administration, supervision, teaching, teacher education* and *curriculum development.* Some members elected to work with this study group because they were concerned with ethnolinguistic minorities within their own countries and with how curriculum and instruction affect these groups, while others were concerned with socio-economic and socio-linguistic minorities who don't succeed in school. Still others were mainly interested in providing multicultural education for middle class and mainstream populations who, they believe, need to understand the complexities and benefits of the multicultural and multilinguistic character of their countries and the world.

As multicultural education must be concerned with shared meanings within and across social groups, the members of this study group sought ways to share different perceptions and understandings of culture and multiculturalism. Some of these differences are represented in the working papers which follow this synthesis. The papers also include issues which the members of the study group did not have time to address.

Through this interchange, we have become aware of very different progress toward multiculturalism, cultural interaction, and multicultural and multilingual education in our various nations. Although we kept our attention on issues of schooling and curriculum it was obvious that our deliberations were strongly influenced by our awareness of sociopolitical and economic factors often external to the control of the educational establishment. Not only do we have less of an impact on political decisions than we might wish, but we also recognize that the minority populations most affected by political decisions should have a much larger role to play in decision making than is usually the case at present. Given the time available, these broader issues received more attention than the specific application within the English/language arts educational context.

We met as a whole group and often in small groups, and time was insufficient for us to work through all the agreements, the disagreements, and shades of interpretation, let alone to order priorities. The achievement of the group, however, was in identifying seven significant issues which are meant to initiate debate and interest.

1. Role of the International Federation for the Teaching of English

Since those involved in the development of this report were drawn predominantly from the Anglo-Saxon, English-speaking world and from wealthy industrialized and powerful nations, we addressed the reasons that IFTE would be interested in discussing multicultural education. We oppose the view that English or the values and beliefs of any dominant culture should be imposed on minorities; rather, we believe that ultimate decision making about multicultural and multilingual education rests with local populations.

In order for the recommendations of the study group to be considered valid, IFTE needs to ensure wider representation from the minority populations of member countries and also from the many other countries of the world where English is a major educational language whether as a first language (e.g. the Caribbean) or a second or other language (e.g., India, Africa, the Philippines, etc.).

2. Definition of Culture

The study group decided that it would be impossible, given constraints of time, to come to a consensus on a definition of culture. The group was working, however, with notions of culture that go far beyond the view that minority cultures are identified chiefly through food preferences, dances and national costumes, maintained as a badge of distinctiveness or as something to share with the majority on special occasions. Nor did the group view English culture as something that schools pour into kids.

We agreed that cultures (and in all our societies they are multifarious) exist for individuals as those individuals participate in them. But the fact of participation also changes culture, so that cultures are also unstable, never established, but always becoming. It is such concepts as these which underlie our concern with multicultural education.

3. Commitment and Power

Multicultural and multilingual education entails the interaction with and understanding of minority cultures and languages in addition to those of the majority. Education, therefore, should be concerned with issues related to English as a second language and bilingualism as well as varieties of English among monolinguals.

Multicultural education, by recognizing the reality of multilingual, multicultural societies, recognizes also the obligation to make provisions for the complexities that arise from them. Teachers must assume the responsibility of respecting cultural diversity and making it an enriching component in the lives of all students. Schools must be organized in such a way as to encourage interaction among ethnic groups and different cultures, so that society as a whole may benefit.

Too often, only lip service is given to the richness of a multicultural society and the importance of understanding and appreciating different cultures, languages and ethnic groups. Too often, little evidence of that richness is found in school programs. Too often, there is little effect on the lives of students. No change can be accomplished in multicultural education without serious commitment by the schools and support of local and federal guidelines and adequate monies. Government commissions in our respective nations have an unhappy history of recommending multicultural efforts and failing to fund them.

4. Students and Curriculum

No group is monolithic. Even such apparently homogeneous groups as the urban or suburban middle class or isolated rural groups contain diversity which may be manifested in socio-economic or attitudinal differences toward learning and child rearing practices. Today most of our schools are faced with broad diversity, including various regional, class and standard varieties of English, as well as regional, class and standard varieties of other languages. The diversity is exemplified by both immigrant and indigenous languages and linguistic mixtures of different kinds, including pidginized and creolized languages. There is often wide-spread code-switching. Such a range of variation in language and culture is a reality which teachers face daily. All those involved in working with students or with the development of multicultural curricula need a more detailed understanding of these variations and their implications for education.

A multicultural curriculum must be developed which helps students draw on their life experiences to find and give shape to their own perceptions and to bring them to articulate expression. Teachers, therefore, need to look at the development of oracy and literacy in a larger context of society and culture than is the case when a prescriptive or normative assumption is made about the role of English/language arts education.

The study group noted that communicatively based approaches to language learning which focus on solving real problems through functional language use seem worthy of further study and support. Such approaches include transactions with people of different ages, experiences, languages and cultures. They may involve the sharing of artistic forms from different cultures in the English/language arts classroom. However, the impact of sharing such forms also needs further exploration. For example, teachers need to consider the ways in which literature and other symbolic forms are used in schools to sensitize and empower students and how they can be used to empower them further. Conversely, it's important to study how such forms have been used to control, diminish and distort human values and intentions.

If we hold this multicultural philosophy of English education, then teachers incur major responsibilities for working effectively with students. They must understand where their students come from and know the backgrounds and language variations they bring to the classroom. Teachers must learn to live with the tensions that come from the interaction of varied value systems and perspectives of multilingual and multicultural communities. But they can't do this alone. School administration, research and teacher education must provide the knowledge base and the emotional and logistic support teachers need.

The group endorsed the view stated in the Bullock Report that students should not be expected to cast off their language and culture upon entering school. This view needs to be understood in relation to all students, not just special populations. In other words, multicultural education isn't to be viewed as a form of remediation limited to ethnic minorities, nor as a superficial awareness of minority cultures. Rather, it must be conceived as a basic component in a well rounded education to which all students have a right.

Students who are fluent in more than one language and are at home in more than one culture are better prepared for participation as adult members of multicultural and multilingual societies than those who are limited to one. Therefore, our concern is with both the majority students, too often deprived of meaningful acquaintance with cultures other than their own, as well as with minority students.

5. Teacher Education

The view of multicultural education suggested by the study group makes great demands on teachers. It is necessary, therefore, to find many opportunities to help the broader public as well as school personnel understand the complexities inherent in teaching and to support teachers through innovative teacher education programs and applied research.

Teacher education must provide the established knowledge about sociolinguistics and social psychology of multilingual and multicultural societies and the developmental and cognitive consequences of different kinds of bilingual education. In addition, since teacher attitudes towards various languages and peoples crucially influence the success of pupils in school and the expectations students have about their power to use language, teacher education needs to help teachers examine the origins of their attitudes towards various languages and cultures.

The study group also strongly recommends that classroom teachers be participant observers and researchers in their own classrooms. Such work enhances the general understanding of multiculturalism.

6. Research

The study group explored innovative research approaches which would encourage collaboration between classroom teachers and theoretical researchers from areas such as anthropology, linguistics, and sociology. Academic researchers need to become more conversant with the real problems teachers encounter in schools in order to understand the questions teachers, administrators and community members raise about the language and cultures encountered in classrooms and school communities. Researchers, teachers, students, and parents have much to learn from each other. This all points to the great need for action research in multicultural/multilingual communities, in classrooms and in schools.

The group noted a number of research studies which would help provide the knowledge necessary for the development of sound multicultural education. For example, we need histories and descriptions of the languages and peoples who come together in the classroom. We also need to understand the range of patterns of acculturation of different ethnolinguistic communities into host countries in order to clarify and explain the differences. We must investigate further the ways in which various host countries acculturate minorities to majority concepts of "success." It is also important to explore the different patterns by which indigenous peoples are dominated in the countries represented and the educational consequences of these patterns. Finally, it is important to have more detailed studies of teacher attitudes toward culturally different students, parents and communities as well as ways of using such findings in teacher education programs.

Research can become a tool for curriculum development. Students can be involved in researching their own communities. They can develop community life histories through student-parent interviews. They can help linguists and teachers collect descriptions of linguistic features of dialect and register differences. Community studies of all kinds are possible as part of a dynamic curriculum in multicultural education.

In order for the kinds of research cooperation suggested here to become a reality, we must review the reward system for researchers interested in doing collaborative and action-oriented research with the schools. Applied research isn't always considered appropriate for academics in universities. Also, there should be rewards for teachers who devote time and effort to such projects. Funding agencies, as well as professional groups, must commit financial support to encourage collaborative action-oriented research.

7. Community/School Cooperation

Minority groups need to be informed about the possible harmful effects which ill-informed educational decisions may have on their children. They need to become aware of their right to a fair education for their children; i.e., one which accepts their language and culture and recognizes their right to maintain them. Minority groups need to feel empowered so they can make their demands of the school system and work with school personnel to help determine what schools can do for them and their children. In this way, minority communities can be drawn into schools. One effect of this will be that school communities, and all of society, will benefit from more active contribution by all of the groups the schools are intended to serve.

At the same time, we must help the majority community appreciate the value of minority cultures so that they don't resent attentions to minority groups. All members of society must be educated about the benefits of multicultural and multilingual education.

Teachers must interact with these various communities whose conflicting interests may be difficult to reconcile. Greater efforts need to be made to help classroom teachers face the difficult task of dealing with the tensions and conflicts that arise. Cooperative planning with community groups is an essential part of this process.

Appendix A
Seminar Participants

Anthony Adams, Cambridge University, Cambridge, England
Peter Adams, Meningie Area School, Meningie, South Australia
Richard Adler, University of Montana, Missoula, Montana, U.S.A.
Richard Bailey, University of Michigan, Ann Arbor, Michigan, U.S.A.
Jenifer Banks, Michigan State University, East Lansing, Michigan,
   U.S.A.
Allen Berger, University of Pittsburgh, Pittsburgh, Pennsylvania,
   U.S.A.
Deanne Bogdan, Ontario Institute for Studies in Education, Toronto,
   Ontario, Canada
Garth Boomer, Curriculum Development Centre, Dickson, ACT,
   Australia
Jill Borthwick, University of Queensland, St. Lucia, Queensland,
   Australia
Robert Boynton, Boynton/Cook Publishers, Sharon, Connecticut,
   U.S.A.
Roger Bresnahan, Michigan State University, East Lansing, Michigan,
   U.S.A.
Syd Butler, University of British Columbia, Vancouver, B.C., Canada
Brian Cambourne, University of Wollongong, Wollongong, New
   South Wales, Australia
L. Jane Christensen, National Council of Teachers of English, Urbana,
   Illinois, U.S.A.
Frances Christie, Deaken University, Victoria, Australia
Merron Chorny, University of Calgary, Calgary, Alberta, Canada
Mary Louise Chubb, Souderton Area High School, Perkasie,
   Pennsylvania, U.S.A.
Patricia Ciancolo, Michigan State University, East Lansing, Michigan,
   U.S.A.
Richard Coe, Simon Fraser University, Burnaby, British Columbia,
   Canada
John Collerson, MacArthur Institute of Higher Education, Milperra,
   New South Wales, Australia

Richard Corballis, University of Canterbury, Christchurch, New
Zealand
Patrick L. Courts, State University College, Fredonia, New York,
U.S.A.
Harvey Daniels, National College of Education, Evanston, Illinois,
U.S.A.
Francine Danis, Our Lady of the Lake University, San Antonio,
Texas, U.S.A.
Pat D'Arcy, Malmesbury, Wiltshire, England
D. F. Davis, Monash University, Clayton, Victoria, Australia
James Davis, Grant Wood Education Agency, Cedar Rapids, Iowa,
U.S.A.
Patrick X. Dias, McGill University, Montreal, Quebec, Canada
David Dillon, University of Alberta, Edmonton, Alberta, Canada
Collette B. Dilworth, Eastern Carolina University, Greenville, North
Carolina, U.S.A.
John Dinan, Central Michigan University, Mt. Pleasant, Michigan,
U.S.A.
John Dixon, London, England
Janice Dressel, Michigan State University, East Lansing, Michigan,
U.S.A.
Charles Duke, Utah State University, Logan, Utah, U.S.A.
David England, Louisiana State University, Baton Rouge, Louisiana,
U.S.A.
Edward Fagan, Pennsylvania State University, State College, Penn-
sylvania, U.S.A.
Sheila Fitzgerald, Michigan State University, East Lansing, Michigan,
U.S.A.
Thomas Franke, Lansing Community College, Lansing, Michigan,
U.S.A.
Peter Fries, Central Michigan University, Mt. Pleasant, Michigan,
U.S.A.
Donald Gallehr, George Mason University, Fairfax, Virginia, U.S.A.
Richard Gebhardt, Findlay College, Findlay, Ohio, U.S.A.
Heather Goodenough, South Australian College of Advanced Educa-
tion, Underdale, South Australia
Warwick Goodenough, South Australian College of Advanced Edu-
cation, Underdale, South Australia
Kenneth Goodman, University of Arizona, Tucson, Arizona, U.S.A.
Yetta Goodman, University of Arizona, Tucson, Arizona, U.S.A.
Elizabeth Gordon, University of Canterbury, Christchurch, New
Zealand
James Gray, University of California, Berkeley, California, U.S.A.
Claudia Haines, Carleton University, Ottawa, Ontario, Canada

Sharon Hamilton-Wieler, University of London, London, England
Jean Handscombe, Board of Education, Borough of York, Ontario, Canada
Richard Handscombe, York University, Toronto, Ontario, Canada
John Harker, University of Victoria, Victoria, British Columbia, Canada
Mary K. Healy, University of California, Berkeley, California, U.S.A.
John Hutchins, Australian Association for the Teaching of English, Norwood, South Australia
Helen Jackman, New Zealand
Angela Jaggar, New York University, New York, New York, U.S.A.
Julie Jensen, University of Texas, Austin, Texas, U.S.A.
Fred Johnson, Papanui High School, Christchurch, New Zealand
Nancy Johnson, Michigan State University, East Lansing, Michigan, U.S.A.
Charlotte Jones, St. Mary's College, Raleigh, North Carolina, U.S.A.
Barbara Kamler, Reverina College of Advanced Education, Wagga Wagga, New South Wales, Australia
Kenneth Kantor, University of Georgia, Athens, Georgia, U.S.A.
Betsy B. Kaufman, Queens College, Flushing, New York, U.S.A.
Julie Kniskern, Glenwood School, Winnipeg, Manitoba, Canada
Nancy Lester, The Write Company, New York, New York, U.S.A.
Jay B. Ludwig, Michigan State University, East Lansing, Michigan, U.S.A.
William Lutz, Rutgers University, New Brunswick, New Jersey, U.S.A.
Ken Macrorie, Santa Fe, New Mexico, U.S.A.
Mary Maguire, McGill University, Montreal, Quebec, Canada
Lucinda Martin, Maple Valley High School, Vermontville, Michigan, U.S.A.
Nancy Martin, London, England
John Maxwell, National Council of Teachers of English, Urbana, Illinois, U.S.A.
John Mayher, New York University, New York, New York, U.S.A.
Scott McNabb, Grand Rapids Junior College, Grand Rapids, Michigan, U.S.A.
Frank McTeague, Board of Education, Borough of York, Ontario, Canada
Joseph O. Milner, Wake Forest University, Winston-Salem, North Carolina, U.S.A.
Diana Mitchell, J. W. Sexton High School, Lansing, Michigan, U.S.A.
James Moffett, Mariposa, California, U.S.A.

Appendix B
Study Group Working Papers

Study Group I

Language, Politics, and Public Affairs

"Language, Politics, and Public Affairs," John Dixon, London, England

"What Do Governors and Educators Recommend to Improve Reading and Writing in the United States and Other Parts of the World?" Allen Berger and Regina Rattigan, University of Pittsburgh, U.S.A.

"The Restructuring of the White Collar Worker and the Restructuring of the Curriculum," Richard Coe, Simon Fraser University, Canada

"Language, Politics, and the News," Peter Evans, Ontario Institute for Studies in Education, Canada

"Language and Student Politics," Betsy B. Kaufman, Queens College, U.S.A.

"The Literacy Crisis That Wouldn't Die," Harvey Daniels, National College of Education, U.S.A.

"Social Change and Language Teaching in Australia," Warwick Goodenough, South Australian College of Advanced Education, Australia

"Years of Living Dangerously: The Corruption of Language and Politics Under (Philippine) Martial Law," Roger Bresnahan, Michigan State University, U.S.A.

Study Group II

Language and Schooling

"Subject Language, Personal Language, and the Construction of Experience," Dennis Searle, University of Alberta, Canada

"New Zealand Speech and New Zealand Identity," Elizabeth Gordon, University of Canterbury, New Zealand

"Patterns of Classroom Discourse," Ken Watson, University of
Sydney, Australia

"Testing and the Notion of Empowerment," Jay Robinson, University of Michigan, U.S.A.

"A New English Curriculum: From Development to Implementation
to Internalization of Theory," Betty M. Swiggett, Hampton,
Virginia, Schools, U.S.A.

"Common Purpose—Divided Way: Some Speculations About the
Fact That Much of What They Were On About at Dartmouth
Is Still with Us," Robert Shafer, Arizona State University,
U.S.A.

"Issues in the Teaching of Writing in American Schools, 1890-1940,"
Kenneth Kantor, University of Georgia, U.S.A.

"Toward a Theoretical Rationale for Progressive Teacher Education,"
John S. Mayher, New York University, U.S.A.

"From Talk to Literacy," Merron Chorny, University of Calgary,
Canada

"Writing Stages: A Developmental Hierarchy," Joseph O. Milner,
Wake Forest University, U.S.A.

"English North of the Border," Sydney Smyth, Scottish Curriculum
Development Service, Scotland

"Language and Thinking: A Perspective for Teaching," Robert P.
Parker, Jr., Rutgers University, U.S.A.

"Standard English: A Discourse Model," James C. Stalker, Michigan
State University, U.S.A.

"The Language of Expert Writing Instruction," Sarah Freedman,
University of California at Berkeley, U.S.A.

Study Group III

Language and the New Media

"Charge to Members of the Study Group," David England, Lousiana
State University, U.S.A.

"Language as Educational Arc," Edward Fagan, Pennsylvania State
University, U.S.A.

"Deleting the Reign of Error," Gordon Pradl, New York University,
U.S.A.

"Writing Across the Disciplines: A Faculty Development Workshop,"
Patrick L. Courts, SUNY at Fredonia, U.S.A.

"A Naturalistic Study of Metaphor in the Linguistic Environment of
Grade One Children," Brian Cambourne, University of Wollongong, Australia

"Word Processing and the Dynamics of Drafting," Richard Gebhardt, Findlay College, U.S.A.

"Redefining Language Learning," Nancy Thompson, University of South Carolina, U.S.A.

"Television's Impact on Literacy Learning," Vernon Smith, Indiana University, U.S.A.

"An American School Uses the Media," Natalie White, Garland, Texas, U.S.A.

Study Group IV

Language, Literature, and Human Values

"Exploring the Territory and Raising Some Questions," Garth Boomer, Curriculum Development Centre, Canberra, Australia

"Virtual and Actual Forms of Literary Response," Deanne Bogdan, Ontario Institute for Studies in Education, Canada

"Literacy, Literature, and Becoming a Person," David Dillon, University of Alberta, Canada

"The Explicit and Implicit Traditions in Literature," Ken Macrorie, Santa Fe, New Mexico

"Narrative Form as Message," Wendy K. Sutton, University of British Columbia, Canada

"The Roots of Response to Literature," Susan Tchudi, Central Michigan University, U.S.A.

"Reader Stances Toward Literary Texts," Nancy Lester, The Write Company, U.S.A.

"Making Sense of Poetry: Patterns of Response Among Canadian and British Secondary School Pupils," Patrick X. Dias, McGill University, Canada

"Reader Response and the Verbal Icon: Implications for English Education," John Harker, University of Victoria, Canada

"Literature: A Participant Sport," John E. Oster, University of Alberta, Canada

"As They Are Taught," James Davis, Grant Wood Education Agency, U.S.A.

"The Value of Logic in Criticism—Especially as It Relates to Drama," Richard Corballis, University of Canterbury, New Zealand

"International Influences in Children's Literature," Patricia Ciancolo, Michigan State University, U.S.A.

Study Group V

Language and Multicultural Education

"Sapir-Whorf Revisit the Classroom," Yetta Goodman, University
   of Arizona, U.S.A., and Mary Maguire, McGill University,
   Canada
"Body Language, Cultural Awareness, and Multicultural Education,"
   James Ney, Arizona State University, U.S.A.
"English Education in a Multilingual World," Richard W. Bailey,
   University of Michigan, U.S.A.
"Dartmouth at the Tertiary Level: A Canadian Experience," Richard
   Handscombe, York College, Canada
"Inner Voices," Claudia Persi Haines, Carleton University, Canada
"Educational Responsibility in a Multilingual School," M. Robert
   Graham, Southeast Missouri State University, U.S.A.
"Puente Project Model," Mary K. Healy, University of California at
   Berkeley, U.S.A.
"Changing Classroom Language," Heather Goodenough, South
   Australian College of Advanced Education, Australia

Appendix C

Meetings of the
International Steering Committee
and the International Federation
for the Teaching of English
1966-2002

1966 — Anglo-American Seminar on the Teaching of English, Dartmouth College, U.S.A.
1970 — International Conference on the Teaching of English, York, England
1980 — International Conference on the Teaching of English, Sydney, Australia
1983 — Seminar on Direction in Research, Montreal, Canada
1984 — Seminar on Language, Schooling, and Society, East Lansing, Michigan
1985 — Nottinghamshire, England
1986 — Ottawa, Canada
1987 — Australia
1988 — United States
1989 — United Kingdom
1990 — New Zealand
1991 — Canada
1992 — Australia
1993 — New Zealand
1994 — United States or New Zealand
1998 — United Kingdom
2002 — Australia

31100053